DATA & ANALYTICS 4.0

DATA & ANALYTICS 4.0

The Future of Work, Privacy and Trust in the Age of Artificial Intelligence

Journel Joseph

Insert Analytics
Washington, D.C. • Boston

First Edition: January 2019

Distributed in the United States and Canada exclusively by Insert Analytics, Inc.

All references and credits appear in the endnotes.

Printed in the United States of America.

ISBN: 978-0-578-43716-3

Author photograph: Kea Taylor
Editor: Lilian N. Blankson
Book Cover and Interior Design: Ghislain Viau

To the Memory of
My Sister Martine
I can still hear her voice say I love you.
Sis, your love continually
keeps me moving forward…

And in remembrance of my cousins
Marie Marthe
&
Charlette

CONTENTS

PART TWO
DECODING DATA AND ANALYTICS

PART THREE
DATA BECOMES AS PREVALENT AS OUR BREATH

PART FOUR
AUTOMATED SYSTEMS, DATA PROTECTION AND PRIVACY PARADOX

PART FIVE
BETTER TOGETHER: HUMANS + MACHINES

PREFACE

Data and Analytics Driven Workforce: Adjust or Give in
(with the Rise of Artificial Intelligence)

"In God we trust, all others must bring data."
—Dr. W. Edwards Deming

We are in the middle of a data and analytics revolution which is driven by digitalization and artificial intelligence (AI). It is disrupting everything in its path and will soon permeate (almost), everything that we do. The speed of change is overwhelming. The timing could not be better to adjust and adapt as companies seek different ways to capitalize on the value of their data. Whether you are interested in learning to respond to market shifts, building a digital mindset, connecting the dots in your own company's data, or simply comprehending the essential principles of data protection and privacy, you are on the right path. This book serves as an instrument infused with forward thinking insights, case studies, relevant frameworks, stories and infographics to help both executives and managers think ahead.

It will also prepare them to navigate the complex challenges as they identify the opportunities that arise. It will provide a comprehensive perspective into the potential risks of data misuse, protection and privacy, digital warfare, as well as exploring the European data privacy policy: General Data Protection Regulation (GDPR).[1] Finally, it will offer 7 key steps for testing your business models by ensuring compliance and embedding dynamic, and proactive privacy principles into your data strategy. I will also bring clarity to the very complex topic of big data that has consumed and revolutionized businesses and governments. This is vital to understand as we cruise into digitalization and interconnected systems.

The Road Map

In this strategic guide, I discuss through real-life and practical examples, the four stages of analytics (descriptive, diagnostic, predictive and prescriptive), the potential impact of systems intelligence, as well as decision-making in today's age of automation and agile management. Further, I explore throughout the text what is described as the TOP techniques (Trends, Outliers, Patterns). These techniques represent the three essential codes of life surrounding data and analytics. They will help managers and executives to navigate unchartered territories as we brace ourselves for a wild ride into the seemingly unknown. Leading companies have attained success by embracing these techniques however, many storied enterprises have also failed and become obsolete by ignoring them. Regrettably, most managers are blind to them which leads to an important question: *Where does your organization stand with mastering the evolution of data and analytics? Or where do you stand?* There is only one way to find out.

Data and analytics can lead to revolutionary and timely insights to saving lives, averting security risks and threats, improving emergency preparedness and enabling better health outcomes. It can also be very critical in enhancing public diplomacy in addition to analyzing and predicting weather and climate variation. Other critical uses could be defined as preventing and mitigating infectious disease outbreaks, unlocking hidden values and gaining competitive advantages. From this perspective, this text enables managers and executives to engage and navigate their way through the ever changing world of data and analytics as it pertains to their organizations. It will also permit them to discern uncertainty and comprehend how to adjust and succeed in the very complex data-driven business landscape. Essentially, they will develop an awareness about the potential impact of artificial intelligence (AI) and the emergence of interconnected systems as we approach the next frontier of digital transformation. This is by no means a quick fix—rather, this will serve as a comprehensive roadmap to guide your path through the golden age of automation. The stakes are high and even personal—but you must embrace data and analytics in order to successfully remain a viable manager with the rise of AI.

Highlight on Artificial Intelligence

"Nothing in life is to be feared, it is only to be understood. Now is the time to understand more, so that we may fear less."

—Marie Curie

As a data and analytics professional, unlike an AI practitioner, my knowledge of this fast developing and disruptive field of technology draws upon the thorough research I have conducted in order to comprehend the nature of this ever evolving phenomenon. In truth, this process has come to influence my assessment, fear and optimism along the way. I am still in the premature stages of learning and figuring out potential AI implications as it applies to my practice in data analytics and data science. It is no secret that artificial intelligence is as good and relevant as the quality of the data that feeds and trains it. This line of thinking fosters my position on speaking about this game-changing technology surrounding data which plays an essential role in its development. To that end, this book will also address the complexities of big data, machine intelligence and offers actionable insights, transformative new ways and the recommendable steps one can take to adjust to the future of the advancing workforce. One more thing. *Do you ever think about your data footprint?*

Beyond

As a point of clarity, I do not focus on programming, mathematics, or statistics in this text. There is a very large body of literature, publications, training sessions and manuals, in addition to varied great MOOC's courses that have already covered these facets and they are all highly recommended. Data and analytics can be comprehended at a necessary level for a manager who does not possess strong statistics and mathematics skills. But, as a point of contention, improving your knowledge of statistics, having a basic understanding of coding and demonstrating a more structured knowledge of data and analytics, could have a positive impact on your career.

Influencers

I do not claim to have originated all of the ideas that are presented in this text. Collectively, they are a representation of the works of varied publications that I have researched and read which have in turn shaped my thoughts, in addition to the various scholars who have trained, mentored and sponsored me. My efforts have been stimulated by over a decade worth of experience as a data geek, applied researcher, consultant, evaluator and as a data and analytics professional. Over the years, I have been repeatedly exposed to breakthroughs, theories, advanced technology, great mentors, data and research gurus, scholars, colleagues and professors who have taught and influenced me. This book is born as a result from a combination of my experiences, thoughts and influences.

The Future of Work: Humans + Machines

The managers, executives and analysts of the future must become comfortable in leading the symbiotic humans-machines[2] driven workforce of the future. They must also have the ability to critically analyze, interpret, review and develop insights from data. They must develop the capability of conducting an in-depth analysis as well as combining actionable insights with experience. Also required is the intuition, creativity of the manager to make thorough and reliable decisions. In short, this guide is for anyone who wants to comprehend the essentials of data and analytics to effectively improve their skillset—be it in the public, nonprofit or private sectors. My hope is that the material covered in this book will lead to a deeper and more complex conversation about the implications of building and implementing AI-driven systems. In addition to entice managers and executives to remain passionate and curious while adapting to the challenges of the data-driven "non-collar workforce" which will result in strengthening their organizations and future-proofing their careers.

PART ONE

THE REENGINEERING BEHIND THE VEIL OF BIG DATA

1

2008: The Year, the Design and the Revolution That Redefined Our Way

"The past, like the future, is indefinite and exists as a spectrum of possibilities."
— Stephen Hawking

The year is 2008. A time in history when a trend would redefine the world as we knew it. How did we get there? It is probably no coincidence that a routine trip to the museum sparked this first chapter and the set up for this book about data and analytics. This gallery of exhibitions is one of the most inspiring settings in the universe. It contains the greatest innovations and countless acts of heroism that have transformed our lives and disrupted conventional wisdom. Standing fascinated in the middle of an exhibition, I felt riveted by an unquestionably revolutionary and transformative moment. I had been transported to an unforgettable past that we celebrate and cherish, yet take for granted today. I surrendered to the stillness of the environment while staring at the images, yet it appeared that they were staring at me. There were generations of people who had masterfully engineered the advancement of communications and technology for modern day. My reflection emerged as I stood in their midst and began to think about the year that set a departure from the past and slowly began to unfold the future.

If I were to ask you to define a moment or event that the year 2008 reminded you of, you would probably point to the great financial crisis or the consequential election of Barack Obama as the first Black president of the United States. Both events were historic and play a significant role in where we are today. 2008 was an incredibly challenging time for Americans and the world at large. Forced into an unforeseen recession, families were crippled by the pain of sudden loss and endless people watched powerlessly as their life-savings vanished, coupled with an unprecedented rate of unemployment. In just a blink of an eye, millions of families had fallen prey to the housing crisis which immediately drove them into poverty. The elections followed and brought hope to the nation and inspired the entire world in the process, but there was more. In some regard, 2008 was a momentous period in time. While incredibly sobering, it also promised great change across the globe. In the middle of the turbulence emerged a brighter future. The inception of the iPhone 3G which came loaded with apps marked the beginning of the rapid pace of the digital revolution. This turning point in big data was unlike anything we had ever seen before with incredibly lasting effects on all of our lives. Just consider the one thing that largely dominates and consumes your daily existence and you will notice that it is linked to the App!

One Download at a Time: The Reinvention of How We Live our Lives

Few, if any, are those that would mention July 2008 as the year Apple founder, Steve Jobs, launched Apple's App Store as a turning point and reinvention of how we live our lives. The first iPhone launched in 2007 was unquestionably transformative. It set the stage for the App Store which was launched with the iPhone 3G (twice as fast at half the price).[3] It sold a million phones in just a weekend, "Compared to the 74 days it took to sell the same amount of the original iPhone,"[4] said Steve Jobs. With a faster processing speed, it also increased in storage size and spearheaded the digital transformation. Additionally, the App Store modernized software development and distribution and quickly set a titanic shift in how customers would interact with their phones. It would ultimately unleash the explosion of big data—just one download at a time.

The iPhone 3G expanded beyond the services of just AT&T in the United States and became available in 25 countries versus just 6, yet it was still being used across the globe. It is safe to say that the world has never been the same since its inception. How so? Bear in mind that in the same year (October 2008) Google introduced the Android Market which later became consolidated as the Google Play Store in the year 2012. It provided a universe of options to select from and a broader reach that was accessible even in the most remote areas of the globe. App Stores have populated on various platforms and the technology has moved beyond mobile to enterprise applications, tablets, personal computers, watches and social media sites such as Facebook Third Party Apps. A 2017 App Annie report revealed that users across the globe had surpassed over 175 billion downloads.[5]

Fast forward to today, apps are used to find love, to network, communicate, study, track health and fitness, order food and even store precious memories. Have you ever experienced or witnessed someone going to a restaurant with friends or loved ones only to pull out their smartphone to snap a dish that looked delicious? The urge to capture the meal and the moment simply cannot be resisted. These pictures of our meals are taken to share with friends or saved as memorable moments. Most of the conversations held today are centered around things we see on our apps (Facebook, Twitter, YouTube, LinkedIn, Instagram, TED, Amazon, Podcast, Netflix, Snapchat, games, current events, news in real time and so on). We laugh, eat, drink, then go off in separate directions. As we head home, we open Spotify or our favorite music streaming service and select a hit song to listen to while we make the drive. If you get the picture, the apps literally become part of our daily routine. It is important to bear in mind as we progress on this journey that the apps are accessible on any tablet, smartphone to anyone regardless of their background, geographic location or cost. You will see why this is so critical a little later.

The Invisibles

Think about this for a moment. The magnitude of the most impactful innovations quite often evades our memory as they become part of the general pattern of our daily lives. They become invisible and their historical reference becomes confined to exhibits halls or galleries at museums. Case in point, we can refer to *paper money* which serves as the eminent symbol of the modern economy and can easily be identified globally. We can also consider the *nail* which enables people to build structures universally or the *telegraph,* a historical breakthrough which completely altered how we communicate information. Something as simple as the 800 toll free number had an indisputable impact on call centers and customer service operations. This also bears reference to the "hidden figures" or invisible hands behind the world's most extraordinary feats. A good example would be Katherine Johnson's influence on space science and computing. She was at the center of the stories of the African-American women, mathematicians or "human computers," who were "essential to the success of early spacecraft."[6] Katherine performed complex calculations (trajectory analysis—landing and return) by hand for the Apollo space mission (the first U.S. manned spacecraft).[7] Her contributions helped NASA pioneer the use of computers in performing complex mathematical models.

One of the most pertinent examples would also be the radio detection and ranging—commonly known as radar system which was originated in the 19th century. "James Clerk Maxwell formulates the electromagnetic theory"[8] that paved the way for Heinrich Heinz's experiment. These systems were popularized in the 20th century, yet in 1935, Robert Watson-Watt was credited for perfecting the technology after demonstrating that radar systems could detect an enemy's aircraft. As a 2008 Wired article described, "It would prove to be a just-in-the-nick-of-time apparatus that helped save Great Britain from defeat in World War II."[9] Having evolved even further, radar systems today enable us to improve how we navigate, observe, forecast the weather, and transform air traffic. The point here is that you do not have to be the originator of a great idea—you can revolutionize pre-existing ones and make your mark in the world. I am certain that you can consider countless other examples. All of this is to say that although the app is personal—like all great discoveries or breakthroughs, it is always available to serve as many people as possible worldwide. As the glue to our fingers, it knows our voices and holds all of our secrets. The wide access and democratization of apps—its broad adoption and usage across cultures and socioeconomic status significantly transforms the world. Evidently, inclusivity makes the apps the most powerful tool in our society. Yes, they come with great challenges—such as heavy usage that could lead to an addiction as well as being prone to manipulation, misinformation, and chronic data misuse.

The Inventive Minds at the Museum: A Journey Through Time

I moved to Washington, DC from Boston a few years ago and I quickly developed a strong passion for the Smithsonian group of museums and unique panoramas. Drawn by the history of innovation and the impactful memories that have transformed humanity, I visit as often as I can. The National Museum of American History became one of my favorites along with the National Museum of African American History and Culture, Freer Gallery of Art, National Air and Space Museum, and the National Portrait Gallery. Quite often, after a hectic day of work, if I do not go for a run on the Mount Vernon Trail or a stroll by the water in Alexandria, VA—I drive to the Smithsonian in DC for a mental break where I often find peace.

One evening, after a routine walk around the Washington monument, I stopped at the National Museum of American History. It always sets my mind spinning into a world of wonder regardless of how many times I visit. I perused the section of inventions and stood in front of the exhibit entitled "*The rise of personal computers in Silicon Valley.*" I reflected briefly on the impact this technology has had on our society and found myself dwelling on those who have changed the course of history through their innovations. They serve as a conduit between heaven and earth. We can generate a long list of those who built and developed state of the art modernizations to advance and solve humanity's most dire challenges. They have unquestionably shaped the world we live in today.

The incredible display on computers dated back to Grace Hopper (hailed as the inventor of computer programing),[10] and later to Bill Gates and Steve Jobs. As I moved around the various exhibits, I pulled out my iPhone and snapped a few pictures before approaching the *Inside Stories*, exhibit with 3 video icons. There was the iconic picture of Steve Jobs suited with a bow tie and arms wide open behind the McIntosh. They were featured on either side and in the middle was a map of Silicon Valley entitled *Why Here? Why Now?* The bottom of the screen read, "Touch an image to view the video. Swipe right or left to scroll to the next." Meanwhile, just a few feet away, a couple with a young boy walked into the booth. The man informed his son that he once owned an Apple Macintosh which debuted in 1984. Next to it was the Xerox Alto (1973)—all locked in the vitrine of history. Behind me, other parents brought their kids to use and play with the ancient computers that were seated on a desk and open to the public.

As I reflected on these inventions, I could not help but think about how far we have come. I walked around and explored various other displays and took a few more pictures including the image of the Intel 8080A 8-bit microprocessor (1974) and read that it is "Generally considered as the first usable microprocessor CPU design, this chip became the central processing unit in traffic lights and the Altair computer."[11] It has since paved the way for the transformation of computing power. Evidently, one cannot think of microprocessors without referring to the Moore's Law, which has been discussed in books, articles, at business events and in academia. Its impact is widely accepted and debated. This would be the perfect example of how some fundamental innovations quickly become invisible, disappear in the background, yet remarkably influence the way our smart devices are powered today.

Throughout the tour after seeing exhibit after exhibit, my mind drifted to thoughts of how technology has impacted my life. It was at that moment when something suddenly hit me, and I wondered how a 4.7-inch (Retina HD display) device could contain and hold almost all of my treasured moments. It plays a significant part in all our lives, and the secret lies in the apps!

How a Design Revolution, Computing Power, and the App Stores Set the Stage for the Proliferation of Big Data

It is increasingly evident that our lives have been shaped by our smart devices. To put this into context, think for just a moment of the impact that apps have in your personal life. Most of the explosive growth of data storage over the past decade can be traced to the rapid growth of computation, interaction, sensationalization and the active usage of our apps. The iPhone Xs and Galaxy Note each came with storage sizes of up to 512GB, compared to the 4GB the first iPhone offered in 2007. In order to measure the sheer magnitude of these numbers which I elaborate on in chapter 8, consider that the very first iPhone with 4 gigabytes of storage had more than 60,000 times the memory of the *Voyager* spacecraft that NASA launched in 1977. The twin spacecraft "Voyager 1 and Voyager 2 have 69.63 kilobytes of memory each."[12] And, they are still flying into space well over 4 decades later. Space travel is fascinating, but let us stop our brief exploration here to go back to the usage of the app. Most users cannot even function with a 16GB memory phone. We require unrestricted access to store our most memorable data. To meet our insatiable demands, the smartphone makers will continue to build devices with increasingly more storage capacity, until it no longer makes economic sense. In turn, companies and special interest groups will promote and advocate for efficient storage management (sort of similar to the energy usage debate over production versus conservation). Until then, we are generating over 2.5 exabytes of data every day.[13] If you are not getting the point yet, you will get a better sense of things in chapter 8, *Big Data Essentials: When Data Becomes as Prevalent as our Breath.*

The Apps: Front and Center in Our Lives

How can we identify 2008 as the year that apps were created when they existed long before then? This is a valid question if we are to consider that the telephone was actually invented in 1876. Fast forward to the progress that has been made over the last decade in telecommunications technology. Just think about WhatsApp, Facebook Messenger, Viber, WeChat, Nimbuzz, and Skype just to name a few, and dwell on how these apps have enabled us to masterfully communicate with our friends, loved-ones and business partners despite their geographic locations. As an example of the magnitude of the usage of these apps, consider that WhatsApp and Messenger users sent an average of 60 billion messages per day in 2017.[14] A CNBC article denoting the impact of Steve Jobs in the "cell phone world" stated that, *"While earlier smartphones had web-browsing capabilities, it was a suboptimal experience. If you wanted to explore the internet, it was generally done from a PC."*[15]

Back to the Future

Indeed, mobile apps have existed in a very basic form since the 20th century. One of the earliest and most notable apps can be identified as the classic game Snake, which was widely popular in the Nokia 3210 or 3310 phone during the late 1990's. Apps started to emerge from early PDAs, generally limited to WAP (wireless application protocol) browsers since bandwidth was limited. A press release dated July 14, 2008, on Apple's website indicated that the iPhone 3G included "800 third-party applications that were then available through the new App store."[16] Although, the first iPhone (2007) and Blackberry (once a leader in the smartphone market), had a few initial built-in applications to interact with. The breakthrough occurred when the ecosystems of Apple and Google opened up to developers to support building third party apps for iOS and Android smart devices.

Data collected from the first iPhone was primordial to influence the design of the iPhone 3G. As Steve Jobs put it, *"We learned so much from the first iPhone, and we took everything we learned and moved to create the iPhone 3G."*[17] A decade later (2018) we are already exploring what Gartner describes as the Post-app era.[18] The key point here is that the apps have already transformed our way of getting things done. The companies that embraced the future thrived while those that did not or were too slow to adjust and collapsed or remained stagnant as a result.

A Quick Reminder: When Incumbents Get Complacent

MapQuest as a web service, played a significant role in the spatial navigation application in the 1990's and early 2000's. It evolved over the years particularly in GPS-enabled mobile phone. The service was exclusively available on Nextel and Sprint from 2004-2005. In 2009, John McKinley penned an article entitled, "*MapQuest: A Symbol of Everything That's Gone Wrong*" in the *Business Insider.* The article captures the essence of the MapQuest app and recounts that the company that was then part of AOL, which is now part of Verizon, *"At some point along the journey, has lost its way."*[19]

Cannot Go Back

It is now inconceivable and extremely difficult for me to even recall the days when I had to find my way by navigating through areas with no street names and dead ends in the darkest hours of the night. How many hours have we all saved with the emergence of apps such as Waze, Google Maps and other real-time navigation systems? We have all been spared the mental anguish from having to stop and ask for directions which would sometimes be sketchy at best. Waze alone has over 100 million users across the globe.

1983! A Time Traveler

What is considered trailblazing? In October 2012, various media outlets (*The Guardian, Business Insider, The Verge, CBS News*), reported that the iconic innovator, Steve Jobs, had conceived and even predicted the App Store, electronic maps and Siri in 1983. It came after a prior article published in *Smithsonian Magazine* on September 2012, covered a rare speech given by Steve Jobs revealing his vision and prediction for the app-driven data world we are living in today. What has really transformed and revolutionized our lives is Steve Jobs and the Apple team's extraordinary design acumen. The simplicity and elegance of the crafting of each product connects with each user. The *Smithsonian Magazine* also reported that Steve Jobs was, "Passionate to the point of obsessive about design…"[20]

From the Love of the Apps Emerges the Data Privacy Conundrum

Our constant thirst to remain plugged increases by the day, consequently, the boundaries of the storage sizes for smartphones keeps expanding to fit our constant data proliferation. This leads to a never-ending quest and a relentless daily pursuit to collect more data. To keep up with the dizzying pace, companies have increased their cloud storage widely beyond the commercial use of cloud services. They have also extended the ability to back up your data right at your own fingertips. These conveniences make it seamless to store the data that is generated from using the apps in our smart devices. The increased accessibility creates the privacy conundrum. Various third-party application developers design their systems with the intent of gathering data from users and these users are often never informed about what types of data is being collected. The sweeping enormity of data collection is at a point where business models are designed to track every move and location of their users. Accessing the data for various business purposes quickly becomes a necessity—a business imperative. This is followed by the wake-up call because these practices raise some very serious privacy concerns. The domino effect causes these same enterprises to suddenly have to re-code their business models because customers do not want their privacy compromised. I will focus more on the challenges and potential solutions to ensure data protection and privacy of your customers or users as well as explore potential impact of regulations in California and Europe in Chapters 9 and 10.

Not All Apps Are Created Equal

How does a marketplace with less than 0.01 percent of financial success in consumer mobile apps dominate our lives to such an extent? Simply put, the power of innovation and breakthrough should not only be measured by its market size. In this instance, the aggregate impact of apps cannot be quantified solely by sheer revenue stream, but rather by how they transform our society. According to Gartner, a significant number of apps are not designed to generate financial returns. *"Less than 0.01 percent of consumer mobile apps will be considered a financial success by their developers through 2018."*[21]

That stated, the App marketplace is expanding rapidly in value. App Annie reported that in 2017 alone, consumers had spent in excess of $86 billion on apps. This translates to over "105 percent growth from 2015."[22] Most of us would agree that the successes of these apps have led the way for significant advances in innovation, disruption as well as digitalization. We can now secure a ride from our smartphone, swipe right or left to find a mate, click to meet new friends, stream our favorite movies or shows, learn new skills and even find jobs—there are apps for all of this. New technology is constantly transforming humanity and the next act will surely bring its share of disruption.

A Bite from the Apple

Apple Inc. has consistently disrupted itself each year and brought us some of the most innovative products since the launch of the classic iPod. It all began in 2001, once the media heralded it as a global success, loyal consumers rushed to follow the new trend. This quickly developed into an obsession for many and it soon became the norm to expect the most recent device to become "outdated" within a year regardless of its cost. Analysts, traders and investors place their bets to buy, hold or sell Apple's stock price on the expectations and preliminary insights ahead of the company's product launch—significant resources are dedicated towards predicting what might come next. Customers worldwide are counting down the date of the next release with great anticipation. Some wake up at dawn on the day of the release, while others make arrangements days before to walk out of the store holding their new device with the utmost pride. It is a magical feeling of privilege.

"It takes a lot of hard work to make something simple, to truly understand the underlying challenges and come up with elegant solutions."[23] —Steve Jobs

In the next chapter, I introduce the TOP techniques which are referred to as trends, outliers and patterns. These simple and familiar concepts drive success for business and lead those that ignore them to failure. They dictate our behaviors, provide cues to what is coming as well as potential risks and opportunities. Although trends, outliers and patterns are vital, they can sometimes go unnoticed to the naive or untrained eye. In 2008, the app marketplace began as an emerging trend that kept us fixated to our smartphones while spending hours on a few of our favorite apps.

The Apps: All-in Our Secrets

Want to go out for a run—*there is an app for that.* Seeking direction to an unfamiliar location—*there is an app for that.* Can't track your sleeping patterns? Want to cope with mental stress? Pray, meditate, learn, find a mate? *There are apps for all of that.* They know our weakness, our pain, our joy and hold our deepest secrets. We become dependent on them to navigate uncharted territory, learn new trends in addition to relevant skills. We conduct our business by using them. They consume our lives, know how we feel and monitor our heartbeats. They spy on us, track us down and connect us with each other simply by clicking or swiping right or left. It actually is not that simple, but you get the picture. Chances are the first thing you do each morning is click on an app and you will continue in this vein throughout the day. You may have listened to a song that put you to sleep or streamed a show or movie the night before. Some (critics, researchers) caution, it is only a matter of time before an addiction ensues and you are literally incapable of functioning without your device.

What Comes Next?

The app stores are filled with a variety of options and it may be hard to find the best niche or the next breakthrough. There are still lots of uncharted opportunities which only require you to look harder or be ready for the next phenomenon. Perhaps it is what Gartner describes as the post-app era. It is critical to be ready for the next big thing which is known as the Internet of Things (IoTs). With smart agents powered by artificial intelligence (AI) that is prone to revolutionize our homes, workplaces, streets and environment, one can only imagine the possibilities. We will be able to operate our smartphones simply by interacting with these gadgets through a simple voice command, option or gesture. This is an important trend to consider as we inch closer to interconnected systems.

Leading the Way

As I previously indicated, trends, outliers and patterns transcend time and surely transform industries. In the digital age, long established companies are being disrupted right from the app stores. While Whatsapp has changed how we communicate, Google Maps, Waze, MapQuest, and Apple Maps have helped us find our way through unfamiliar roads and territories. We rely on YouTube to catch up on past events, watch our favorite videos and consume content that inspires and moves us. We stream our favorites songs through Spotify, iTunes, and Pandora while Netflix revolutionizes how we pay for and watch movies, documentaries and television series. One of the most important lessons to remember in this complex business landscape is that things move and change rapidly—so rapidly that a brilliant and groundbreaking idea for the next big thing could soon be dated before dawn—so to speak.

So, What Happened After the Museum

Succeeding in the era of smart automation or any technology requires innovation and dedication. As I left the museum on that evening, I felt motivated and empowered. I became more and more convinced that the power of those game changers that have transformed our lives was derived from their deep-rooted belief of making the world a better place, not destroying it. I exited the museum, walked to my car and drove away. On my way home, I stopped midway at a Starbucks and ordered a Grande Caramel Frappuccino and paid with my Starbucks app. Doing so earned me a few stars. I went back to my car, clicked on Spotify to listen to the hits du jour and drove off. Shortly after, a friend visiting from out of town called via Google Voice and asked if I was available to meet up for dinner. Agreeing to do so, I asked her to select a restaurant, reserve a table and text me the address to pick her up later. I would have to change my original plan of streaming a rerun of *Person of Interest* on Netflix about the Machine that "sees everything." I arrived home, relaxed for about an hour and began writing this story on the Notes app on my iPhone. With my time being up, I readied myself to hit the road again. I entered the address in Waze and selected the best route to get there. My friend had made a reservation at Le Diplomate using her OpenTable app. As you can see, all happened rather quickly in a normal and seamless way—thanks to the apps.

The coolest and most remarkable thing about the apps, is that someone living in Accra, Ghana; Nairobi, Kenya; La Paz, Bolivia;

Port-au-Prince, Haiti; Cambridge, MA; London, United Kingdom; Silicon Valley, CA; Birmingham, AL; Quebec, Canada; Toulouse, France; Jakarta, Indonesia; Tokyo, Japan; Hanoi, Vietnam or any developing country, city or any remote corner of the world with access to a smartphone phone can experience and use the very same apps. They can use a dating app to find love, make a reservation at an Airbnb, tweet, share posts on Facebook, Instagram, Snapchat or YouTube about their most cherished memories. They can take a course on Coursera or LinkedIn Learning regardless of their social status, geographic location or how much they paid for their smartphone. The app does not discriminate, care about your education level, where you live or even who you are. As long as you have access, it belongs to you. It is unrestricted; making it transformative, definitively revolutionary—and also frightening.

The Next Frontier of Innovation

Depending on your business model, you most likely do not need an app, but you need to investigate built-in systems that you can plug into in order to grow your enterprise. If your business requires that you build an app, dive into the marketplace's statistics to detect emerging trends, potential outliers, and comprehend the current patterns. Technology is so ingrained in everything that we do that it is sometimes taken for granted. The power of the app lies in its ability to improve our lives as well as complicate them. It influences our behavior as we get addicted to our smart devices. You might be one of those who perceive the future as being a bit depressing with the advent of robots and AI, or like me, you might have the confidence that *humans are underrated* in discussions about the future. Humans are indeed vulnerable to the automation that will cause substantial changes in our lives. What is coming is unlike any disturbance we have ever seen before—a titanic shift that could lead to gigantic disaster or a huge transformative gain for humanity. I am betting on the latter.

The Arrival of AI

The evidence of the ultra-fast pace of computing power was laid out by Greg Brockman, the co-founder and CTO of Open AI (a non-profit company with a mission to build safe AI systems), during an interview on Bloomberg Technology on June 26, 2018 with Emily Chang. He indicated that the amount of computing power has grown 300,000 times over the past 6 years.[24] The interview was conducted following his testimony to the United States Congress on artificial intelligence (AI). Upon first watching the interview, I thought I misunderstood his explanation, and listened to it twice more still unable to believe what I had heard. I later searched for his testimony to the U.S. Congress and read it. He clearly stated, "This growth is significantly faster than the historical driver of hardware progress, Moore's Law, which had an 18 month doubling period (a 12x increase over the same period)."[25] This could be considered frightening, astonishing or impressive. He compares the phenomenon to the equivalent of having your smartphone battery life go from "One day to 800 years worth of charge. In 5 years from now, it equates to 100 million years of battery life."[26] He also revealed that their study showed that this trend would only continue to accelerate.

I want to underline that as we are building the future, we must consider the ripple effects of our algorithms, the quality of data that we use to train artificial intelligence and the awareness that our biases could alter the course of history for generations to come. A rejection in the form of a human "revolution" against machines and the companies that built them will soon emerge. Experts in AI are pushing for uncharacteristic expressions of caution in developing and implementing AI-driven systems to ensure that the technology is beneficial rather than destructive towards humanity. In the process, it is important to keep in mind that the success or failure of a product or service depends on its adoption. If customers or users do not embrace a product or service and understand how it will improve their lives, humanity, the future or an organization, it is most likely that it will not be successful or achieve its fullest potential. This has always been the key differentiator between innovators that failed and those that prospered and ultimately, those who made it to the exhibit halls of the museums. The future is and will always be human-driven, supported and enhanced by intelligent machines, not the other way around. Again, do not underrate humans. None of this is to say that AI will not cause damage, it will—to an extent beyond our prediction. Since we are still in the early phases and do not know what to expect in 10 years from now, we can only conceive and design projects to unlock opportunities and ensure that AI is accessible to all. As we move to the next frontier, the companies that build and implement AI-powered systems in order to encourage and augment human capacity, will make life better for its customers and be well-positioned to thrive in the future. AI is refreshing. It has great potential, but also comes with risk. In short, it is an unavoidable juxtaposition of extremes—loaded with indispensable promise and unpredictable complexity.

PART TWO

DECODING DATA AND ANALYTICS

2

Know What to Know: The TOP Techniques (Trend - Outlier - Pattern)

"There is some sort of commonality in the emergence of great business leaders; the bold ones tend to rise during a time of crisis. What many defined as a challenge seems to offer rare opportunities for them to thrive. Simply put, they develop the ability to foresee things that others are unable to even imagine."

— Journel Joseph

Data has changed every aspect of business and society in a fundamental way unlike anything we have seen previously. The stakes are high, and the challenge is to figure out how these profound changes will impact your career. To be prepared for the future of the work environment, executives and managers must develop the ability to read, interpret, organize and manipulate data in order to answer the questions that are relevant to their business operations or programs. The *how* remains the blind spot that must be quickly addressed, as we approach the next frontier of digital transformation. In the future environment of business, managers will be expected to interact and work harmoniously with machines, as artificial intelligence (AI)—the trend du jour, rapidly seeps into everyday life. What then becomes pertinent is where to begin.

Big Data and Advanced Analytics: A New Era?

One of the key challenges surrounding the use of data and analytics in the 21st century closely relates to knowing how to effectively connect the dots in addition to comprehending the benefits and risks that come with it. Evidently, traditional systems or tools are ill-equipped to process and analyze the unprecedented amount of data that is constantly flooding our daily lives, businesses and government agencies. I discuss some of these opportunities and limitations in chapter 8, *Big Data Essentials: When Data Becomes as Prevalent as our Breath.* Despite the substantial constraints most companies face—conducting data analysis has been the driving force to deriving insights, uncovering hidden opportunities, developing different therapies to save lives. And in some cases, it has been used to cause harm (yes, this story also has its dark side). Most importantly, it has led to significant breakthroughs in various industries and has also contributed to the understanding of population growth. Additionally, it has facilitated economic development for centuries. These include the first reported U.S. census which was conducted in 1790 as mentioned in chapter 7.

Data and Analytics 4.0?

The title of the book, Data and Analytics 4.0 effectively draws attention to the evolution of data and analytics over the years—from human computers performing manual, tedious, repetitive and rule-based tasks to advanced analytics powered by AI, automation, cognitive computing systems, special tools and methods (as discussed in chapters 4, 5, 8 and 9).

These complex systems, (artificial intelligence and robotic process automation—commonly known as RPAs) are changing the way enterprises operate and compete. As a result, devising an efficient implementation strategy remains a serious challenge for most businesses and government agencies. With that said, I would like to highlight an important lesson that I have learned from professor Carsten Kowalczyk (one of the most cited International Economists who also served as my thesis advisor at The Fletcher School). He often cautions that it is important to know and be very clear about what you are not going to do, write or talk about. He would argue that these steps are essential to avoid being bogged down in the mud. This is a valuable reminder as our daily lives are inundated with big data. From that viewpoint, I want to stress that I am not particularly interested in identifying or defining eras or even focusing on the historical aspects of data and analytics in this book. To be clear, regardless of the time frame or years that you select as a specific period, especially any cutoff dates that may suggest when analytics 1.0 and 2.0 began and ended, would remain solely arbitrary choices. The dates in question would vary depending on whom you asked. And this could lead to fundamental questions surrounding the foundation for such a classification and may seem by necessity to be an oversimplification. Nonetheless, the numbering is helpful and could serve by placing things into a broader perspective—namely assessing just how far we have come. What is vital to bear in mind is that the use of data and analytics has become a business imperative. It is indispensable in driving decisions across all industries and sectors (I illustrate this in chapters 1, 3, 4, 5, 7, 8 and 9). With these initial points, my purpose is to help you understand how to effectively navigate the unchartered territories of our modern day's age of data and analytics by using practical cases and scenarios.

Before moving any further, I would like to credit Thomas Davenport who has written extensively about the evolution of analytics (3.0 and 4.0). His book, Competing on Analytics, which is co-authored by Jeanne G. Harris, serves as an excellent resource for detailing the evolution of analytics.

From the Ground Up: Turning Data into Insights

This is where everything comes together—the process of turning data into insights to make smarter and faster decisions. Let us explore behind the scenes—that is, what must happen to conduct data analysis. The first order of business is to give your analytics project a purpose, then begin with a preliminary examination and assessment of your company's data to create a road map of where you want to go. Analytics cannot be conducted in a vacuum — thus the importance of having a use case (demonstrated in the infographic on page 38), asking relevant questions and designing a plan of action is a necessary step. That said, you must understand the data collection process and assess how reliable, accurate and relevant the data is to support the purpose of your analytics project. Define first what type of data is available to you. Next would be determining how and when the data was collected. As you become consistent with this goal, it is essential to become familiar with the types of data required to generate your analysis. You must be comfortable with classifying your data through quantitative and qualitative methods (as discussed in chapter 6). As you will soon discover, you use insights generated from data every day to make life decisions—unless your life is being led by others. Consider this form of analytics as a journey and adventure where you will make mistakes then, continuously reflect and learn from them. In the end, the decisions you did or did not make, and the path you did or did not take contribute in defining where you are today.

While this is all great in theory, knowing what to look for in your data is still not so obvious and could be a serious hurdle. I will address how to approach this process and will share some illustrations and real-life applications. As a guiding principle, it is important as a manager to become familiar with what is happening in your industry and to measure how your brand is perceived beyond your day-to-day operation.

Next Step

Let us assume that as a division manager, you have already mastered the workings of your industry. The next step would be to read, understand, interpret and translate your data into valuable insights. It is critical to be proficient enough to help bridge the gap between the data and analytics professionals and your organization's leadership. Think of your role as a translator in that regard. Though this is necessary as a baseline, the most significant part of the process is to consider the relevant and specific context through which your data should be analyzed. It is also important to explore a few pertinent use cases (explained in the next section), as you embark on the process. From this perspective, you must understand that the real dynamics that are required to prepare you for your journey into data and analytics involves planning, curiosity, critical thinking, judgment and commitment.

So, Where to Begin?

A simple action is to identify a starting point, this could mean putting the emphasis on scanning the market place for untapped opportunities, identifying some key questions, and assessing how they apply to your data.Whether it is exploring how customers use or view your product, the brand or their perception translates to what is being said about it on social networks or review sites. In today's age of data and analytics, you cannot afford to *not* know how your service, product or brand is being perceived. Then, you may ask *how*? Well it depends. As a basic principle, it could all begin by adopting a routine strategy to monitor and assess your company's social media pulse and unearthing the insights that are buried in unstructured piles of data shared by your users or customers. This can be done by analyzing tweets and Facebook and Instagram posts for example as well as reviews to capture relevant data on your customers' state of mind and perception of your brand. If your company is not active on social media, consider following brand influencers and exploring content related to your industry's growth trajectory, products or services. Then, ask your customers directly by conducting interviews, focus groups or surveys. I discuss these methods of data collection in chapter 7. Regardless of the method that you choose, it is vital to consider that you have to be where your users or customers are.

"... The phenomenon that is social media has shifted the balance of power to consumers, opening up opportunities as well as increasing organizational risk. The good news is that social listening is valuable for both the upside and the downside."[27] PwC

"Powered in part by the continued ubiquity of the smart-phone—now firmly in the hands of over 87 percent of the U.S. adult population—social media reached about 177 million people each week on average in the third-quarter of 2016."[28] Nielsen

In short, these strategies (taking the pulse of social media or asking your customers directly), will help you understand the purchasing or usage behavior of your consumers, and track emerging trends, detect outliers and identify patterns.

Evidently, it would take time, creativity, strategic planning, dedication, a great dose of curiosity and hard work to adjust to new ways of thinking. Once you figure your way through the learning curve, you will wonder how you ever performed these functions without thinking about trends, outliers, and patterns in the daily operations of your business. To reach that level, you must stick to the process to connect the dots and trust that this process will become a normal part of your business practice. If you want to advance to the next level, it is essential to stick with a simple use case, and 1 to 3 questions that would enable you to grasp the usage of your organization's data and business value to generate actionable insights.

A Note About Use Cases

I will be using the term *use case* repeatedly throughout this chapter and beyond. Coined by Ivar Jacobson[29] in the 1980's, the concept has been instrumental in helping to guide software development, systems engineering, complex applications, and to process framework, as well as model planning and design. In the IT and software development world, a use case delineates the purpose of a system in terms of the ways a user will interact with it. This concept can be very useful in managing many kinds of projects and is considered essential for a manager's toolbox. As the authors of a 2014 *Harvard Business Review* article entitled, "Sometimes the Best Ideas Come from Outside Your Industry" have put it: "Bringing in ideas from analogous fields turns out to be a potential source of radical innovation...The greater the distance between the problem and the analogous field, the greater the novelty of the solutions."[30] To address this term in more detail, I developed a framework (5 stages) to help you understand and design a Use Case. So, what might a "Use Case" look like? And why it matters. Let's look at the process of getting there.

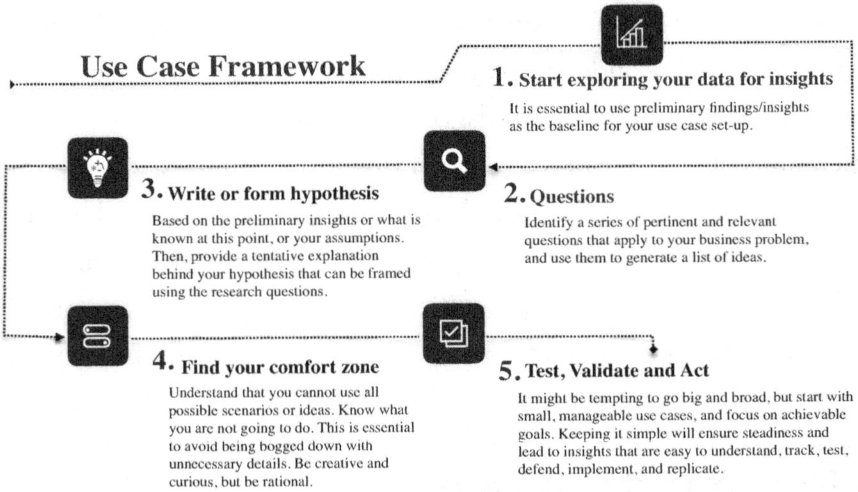

Developing a use case should start with asking the simple and fundamental question, "*What is the purpose of this project/product/effort?*" You will be surprised to realize how plans will become more targeted, goals redefined, and how a sequence of actions will be followed more clearly with this simple rubric. When it comes to data exploration, consider these series of questions: *Why are we looking at this data?"* and *"What questions do we have?"* More importantly, we can start with *"What I know now, what do I need to know/learn and do to advance?" "How do we proceed to acquire the information required?" "How can we utilize the information obtained to increase our efficiency?" "What is the next question we should consider asking, and how do we secure the answers?"* If the use case is incoherent or lacking in foundation, contemplate asking more questions. This will offer the opportunity to reduce spending on unnecessary initiatives, save time and move forward with relevant use cases that are essential in optimizing how a business performs.

The TOP Techniques

Developing an awareness about trends, outliers and patterns (let's call them the TOP techniques), in your data could help you go beyond the basic requirements of your function and create impactful stories about your customers, programs, products and brands. This practice will quickly become second nature as you continue to improve your craft. I refrain from getting into statistics in this introduction; however, truly mastering these techniques will require some basic knowledge of statistics, or a partnership with an able analyst.

Trends

"...Understanding and mapping trends, would give consumer companies a starting point for understanding which trends could have the greatest effect on their businesses."[31] McKinsey

Analyzing trends can also aid in predicting the future path of sales, developing new products, and launching more targeted

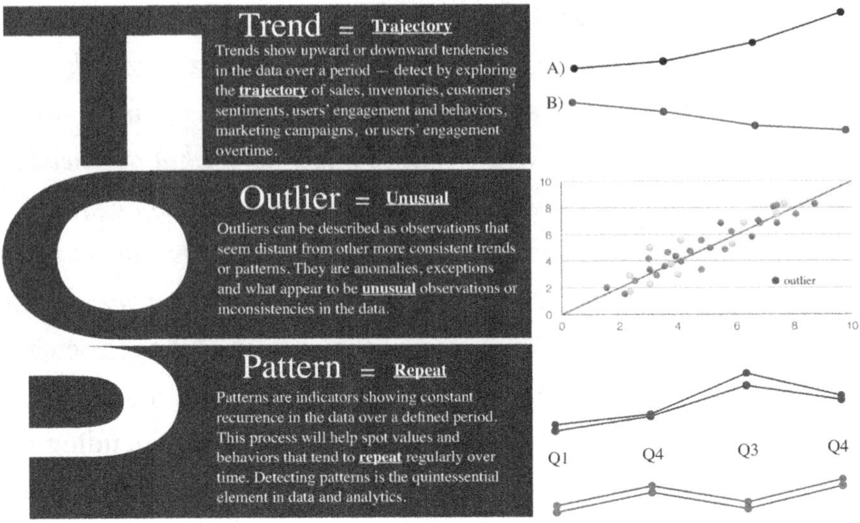

marketing campaigns. The process of understanding and applying trends to gain insights from data can serve as a strong differentiator in how to compete in a specific market, and is paramount in predicting the future. As you reach a level of comfort in analyzing data, it will become a normal process to foresee the trajectory of the market and eventually better position your enterprise to take advantage of relevant insights and emerging trends.

Outliers

"An outlier is an observation which deviates so much from the other observations as to arouse suspicions that it was generated by a different mechanism."[32] Hawkins, D.

Conducting an analysis on any type of data sets can reveal outliers. However, dealing with unusual values, such as outliers, can be rather challenging. The term outlier can be described as an observation that seems distant from other more consistent trends or patterns. Simply put, they are anomalies or exceptions from what appear to be unusual observations or inconsistencies in the data that deviates from the general pattern.

It is important to understand and interpret the causes of potential outliers, which requires taking a deeper look. Are they one-time events? Do they dictate a reporting, sampling, or computation error in the data—chance or natural occurrence, or do they simply suggest a potential shift?

Outliers must be treated and handled with attention, and are sometimes inevitable, but are important to investigate to gain a broader context of the data and to understand the underlying complexities and explanations behind these exceptions and anomalies.

Patterns

Although all 3 levers are essential and relevant—I want to emphasize that the ability to detect patterns is an essential component in data and analytics—and in (almost) every decision we make in life. Every single customer, for example, develops patterns that could be used to predict their potential purchasing behavior. If you could decode the patterns in their activities, you would be able to use that information to model their possible behavior—eventually anticipate and corner where the market is going. Ultimately, you would offer them what they would need even before they know it. Mastering this code will enable you to find a needle in a haystack. So, how these techniques apply in real-life? Time to find out.

A Journey: Turning Trends, Outliers and Patterns into Opportunities

To embark on this journey, I propose keeping it simple. You will need to change the way you think and work in two basic ways: (1)

You are going to adjust your work process by devoting 15-20 percent of your time to working smarter by taking an audit of your organization's data and identifying what is available to you. (2) During the course of that time, you will practice three basic observation-based techniques. They can be referred to as the essential codes of data and analytics (described as the TOP techniques): Trends, Outliers, and Patterns. These are the formulas—three common and familiar words—fit for the digital age. They represent the key drivers that managers should be able to detect and measure with some level of comfort in their budgets, revenues, company's data, fundraising activities, sales data and product development. It is important to take them to heart and make them a quintessential part of your business operation. Their applications will be examined throughout the book and they are critical to help detect root cause of security breaches, drop in sales—spot contaminated data, and identify potential disruptors in your industry—and help you to remain in control, and calm in the trenches. Significant consequences—both positive and negative—are linked to these three metrics, even when you are not paying attention. Many leading companies have failed and become obsolete by ignoring them. As a result, they become the fallen victims of innovation and disruption.

Perspective: What Does It Take?

"I have no special talent. I am only passionately curious." Albert Einstein

Being curious is essential and the primary prerequisite for developing a keen interest in making data and analytics part of the journey to future-proofing your career and becoming prepared for the workforce of the future. As previously stated, one of the primary goals of this book is to help you as a manager initiate how to explore your way towards data and analytics. It is not going to be immediately clear as you begin, but you will gain confidence with practice and incremental progress. This process is designed as an initial stage that will enable you to follow the trends and turn insights in your favor, move with speed and confidence in a very complex business landscape. Although managers can learn how to eyeball trends, outliers and patterns after plotting the data, they should opt to perform these assessment techniques by using computer assisted analytics tools to analyze and visualize data.

Gaining an Edge with Data and Analytics in a Volatile Business Landscape

To get started, the following scenario is a case that combines a common reality that many retail companies have experienced over the past few years. Few manage to come out, some are still struggling, and others have gone out of business. This is an illustration of a company that is still in a lethargic state. First, understand clearly that data matters. According to a *MIT Sloan Management Review* (2017) publication, the manager's ability to formulate, articulate or frame a problem statement is primordial and often underrated.[33]

Scenario: Holla & Co.

As noted earlier, there are countless companies that are now defunct, or nearly so for failing to understand and foresee the rapid changes of digital transformation. Consider the following scenario with a national retail company—let's called it Holla & Co. The company has seen a downward trend in its northeast region market resulting in a drop in its revenue over the past eight quarters. To address the recurring pressure on revenue, initial interventions led to reducing prices to entice customers back, but the downward trend continued, which seemed to indicate a larger threat that required the senior executives to address immediately. As a typical survival response, the company opts to arrest the downward spiral with cost cuts strategy. This helps reduce loss, but the problem is that customers appear to have already lost interest in the company's products. This loss of interest has consequently dragged down Holla's total revenue and the early decisions did not reduce the downward spiral.

Spinning Out of Control

As time passes, the decline begins to generate deep worry and frustrations among the top executives. The problem seems acute. This prompts the company to launch an in-depth study to investigate what seems to be causing the downward spiral with no end in sight. As part of the process, the data and analytics team sift through the company's data to gain insights that will inform their next steps. They design a comprehensive plan to assess the underlying factors that might have caused the drop in revenue. In this effort, speed is of the essence with very little room for errors. The team enlists managers from various business units to provide some insights—assuming that they are closer to the data of their customers. The initial assessment leads to the following questions as the guiding framework to reflect and inform potential use cases:

1. Is there any available data and preliminary findings that might offer an accurate, reliable and relevant insight to inform the investigation?

2. Does the company have an established data strategy to harness and optimize insights?
3. What are the key indicators of the declining trend, and what are the core drivers that are causing the shift in the Northeast market?
4. Are there new entrants in the market, or unforeseen patterns that are driving the decrease in revenue?
5. Did they overlook the outliers?
6. Were there changes in the buying patterns of customers over the past few years and did the organization fail to predict the shift?
7. What are the implications for the company's long-term viability in the identified markets and beyond?

Data-driven and Agile Manager

Data provides a viable advantage in uncovering your customer's behavior. To be precise, determining what they need and want in order to create value for your organization. Now, stop and step back for a moment and imagine your role as a manager before the problem became acute for the retail company Holla & Co. As we approach the next section, I want to underline that staying informed on what is happening in your industry could be valuable in helping you follow the data. In a world consumed by big data, it is important as previously indicated to have a starting point—it is indeed a journey.

Industry Spotlight Matters

Let us assume you have developed a routine to stay connected to the evolving trends that are shaping the retail industry over the last few years. You would have ideally read reports from Nielsen, and the National Retail Federation (NRF) on millennial consumer trends. One of the reports indicated that the millennial population is growing and thriving in purchasing power and that they are willing to pay higher for better quality, eco-friendly and sustainable goods. The point here is that as a manager, it is vital to understand that the insight that could spark innovation could come by way of staying connected and reading about industry emerging trends and patterns. That said, you would have seen the writing on the wall and would have been prepared to argue that pricing was not the sole factor causing the decline in revenue. At this stage, you could develop a hypothesis based on your assumptions, but informed by industry reports that need to be tested or proven. You sensed that your company did not have a strong data structure or ecosystem that was tracking customer engagement by demographics in those specific markets. As a result, you decided to be proactive.

Managers oversee the product's life cycle and are closest to their customers' data. It would be a natural choice for them to be more engaged in the data analysis related to their products, and customers. Let us say, you plotted and mapped out (using a data analytics tool, like Tableau, SAS or SPSS), your company's sales data for respectively four, eight and twelve quarters, then combined it with behavioral data, along with the U.S. census demographics trend data by region. Your "use case" would have been to assess whether or not there was a correlation between the downward trend in revenue due to demographic change or the customer's spending behavior by connecting the dots.

Then, a Data Twist

You detected an important trend—that is, the census data indicated an upward trend in the millennial population of the Northeast region over the past 5 years. You also uncovered that the core demographics of your business was stagnant. These minor hints would have provided relevant insights and your "aha moment". It is after all, important to practice the art of discovering little hints in your data before diving in until you discover bigger hints that will become tested and reliable insight.

The findings revealed a shift in the demographic and the purchasing behavior of the customers suggests that something must be done, otherwise Holla & Co will run the risk of being disrupted. What should happen?

The drive toward data and analytics is inevitable and inherent to the survival of a business. As a manager, you serve as the bridge point between your customers and the organization. You must find and articulate your voice and be proactive in using the data of your customers to inform your next steps. There is some sort of commonality in the emergence of great business leaders; the bold ones tend to rise during a time of crisis. What many defined as a challenge seems to offer rare opportunities for them to thrive. Simply put, they develop the ability to foresee things that others are unable to even imagine. This shows how imperative it is to prepare managers for big data's inevitable effects on their success or failure. Companies with the right workforce will be better positioned to maintain a competitive advantage in the digital age and those that do not may become obsolete. Any delays in adapting to this fast-changing business landscape will further complicate a company's position in the market. One thing is clear; companies of the future will need to enhance a data driven winning culture and bolster the capabilities of a manager to improve productivity and change their businesses.

Balancing Act

I want to highlight that in many cases, managers might have seen the edge of the cliff approaching. The attempts to share their insights with the company's leadership were unsuccessful. Their companies eventually collapsed. The managers are often powerless to act—their voices remain silenced until it is simply too late. This is a scenario that we can clearly envision. To succeed in this complex business landscape and stay ahead of the curve, companies must establish preconditions to embrace, empower, and help managers unearth and share insights. This can be implemented though innovation labs supported by senior executives—deploy internal resources and build capacity to respond swiftly to disruptions and facilitate innovation from the bottom up that will drive a culture of continuous transformation.

Suited Up to Lead

Kenneth Chenault, the former CEO of American Express Co., is a case we can consider where demonstrating foresight, strategic thinking, and intuition helped save an important division of the company. Amex Travel Related Services Co. nearly collapsed in the early 1990's and Kenneth Chenault was instrumental in not only helping to revive, but also reinventing it in the process. He later became the company's chairman and CEO, and successfully led Amex and its employees to significant and sustained growth over the years. Retired in February 2018, after 17 successful years,[34] the stalwart CEO was one of the most effective global business leaders throughout his tenure and led Amex to an extremely volatile global landscape. Great achievements are guided by some key principles, such as proactivity, execution and foresight. All of these attributes can be accomplished through the effective use of data.

And...Ride on the Trend, Outlier and Pattern

Perfecting your eye for data and analytics will ultimately requires a deeper knowledge of statistics and hours of practice. As you go through the process, you might find it helpful to discuss your observations and initial findings with your team, other managers and particularly data and analytics professionals. Data analytics is a team affair. Do not underestimate the value that the TOP techniques might add to your business operation. In the data-driven marketplace, speed is paramount. Understanding the key indicators that trigger the decline in revenue could lead to the need to refine inventories, adjust marketing strategies, and much more.

Back to Holla & Co!

The company will soon discover that competitors offer more fitted solutions to customers and that new players have entered the market with better offerings. And they did not build an efficient and intelligent system to detect trends, outliers and patterns in a rapidly changing marketplace—therefore, they are ill-prepared to respond fast enough and adjust to changes. What should happen? At this point, Holla & Co has few options, including: 1) exit the Northeast region market, 2) downsize to few strategic and limited number of stores and focus on improving the experience with fast quality and premium service—suited for the modern-day customer, 3) acquire a competitor or startup. A strategic acquisition would enable Holla & Co to keep up with the changing customer landscape and remain viable in a fast growing demographic group, and important market. In subsequent chapters, you will discover how efficient and intelligent use of data and analytics will help devise relevant solutions to future-proof your company.

What Is Most Important?

Despite the limitations of managers to perform certain in-depth data and analytics operations, a simple awareness such as being able to relay and translate the challenges to senior executives and data scientists could be vital in enriching their roles.

Unlocking these analytical codes will allow the manger to leverage data to optimize inventory and focus on purchasing or developing products or services with higher profit margins during specific times—thus translating insights into opportunities. The TOP techniques embedded in advanced analytics could arm the manager with the right intelligence to cut product categories with lower demands as well as predict when they might need to cut or increase inventory.

Trends, outliers, and patterns (TOP) offer ways to grasp and even master the fundamentals of data analysis techniques. This requires early and holistic groundwork in order to consistently measure your enterprise's fitness and historical data along these core principles or attributes. When applying the TOP techniques, it is important to take advantage of lessons learned by other companies—in the next chapter, I explore some of the underlying factors behind disruptive changes into the technology industry over the past decade. These codes (trends, outliers, and patterns) can reveal distinctive insights that will help to understand your market, help foresee changes in real-time, stay proactive and relevant—in addition to optimizing business models and connecting the dots to the discovery of how the world around us works and evolves.

Reflections: Assessing your TOP Fitness Using the Following 9 Questions

1. What do you know about your industry and your market?
2. Do you foresee any imminent threats to your industry over the next two, three or five years?

If you do not know enough about your industry and market, use reliable data and the following questions to find out:

3. How many competitors are in your market?
4. How would you define and segment your competitors? New entrants? Modern or new age incumbents? Traditional incumbents?
5. What seems to be the current trends or patterns in your industry?
6. Are there any outliers?
7. What are the demographics trends of your customers and/or users?
8. If your company is operating in different markets or serving different demographic groups, what are some of the tendencies and patterns for each market and demographic group?

9. How would you measure or rate barriers to entry in your industry?

3

Connecting the Dots

"You can't connect the dots looking forward; you can only connect them looking backwards. So, you have to trust that the dots will somehow connect in your future."
—Steve Jobs

If you are not connecting the dots, they will be connected on your behalf. It could be competitors for example, who are connecting them to take you out of the market. Managers should have a systematic method for identifying trends, outliers and patterns in their business operation. As previously demonstrated, trends, outliers, and patterns provide a clear baseline and a framework to collectively see the writing on the wall of a fragmented and turbulent market landscape.

Looking Backward and Forward: What It Takes

Connecting the dots backwards then forward can achieve unprecedented performance and lead to discoveries when properly executed. Here is what to look for in the process:

Backwards: refers to that which is known, lived and seen. In the process, keep in mind that there could be more than what is known to explain what happened. Consider confounding variables such as hidden factors or invisible attributes that contribute to the known outcome. Looking backward can be a flawed process if you focus on using the data to justify your hypothesis. It is important to pay attention to the events or data points that could refute it as well. Doing so will enable you to move forward with descriptive information adequate enough to assess what happened. Then, the next step would be to understand why it happened—the diagnostics (discussed in chapter 4).

Forward: takes into consideration the unknown. Let us consider this as the process of using models to make predictions or forecast the future. This can be quite complex due to unpredictable events, uncertainties, and surprises such as the case of force majeure beyond what is predictable. It is also important to consider the possible surprises and outliers that could disrupt your prediction. As you proceed, it is critical to explore what the model either did not or could not foresee. The model is as good as the data you feed it, yet also limited due to the assumptions that it is based on. Be aware of bias, inaccuracies and fallacy in your reasoning or assertions. Simply put, you must pay attention to the potential outliers or unforeseen events that could significantly change the trajectory of your predictions. It is vital, as previously indicated, to build a system that is apt to adjusting to any potential variations in real-time. I address these concepts in chapter 4, covering the four stages of analytics.

Only the Bold Will Survive: Insight into the Tech Sector

Let us take a look at the disruptive changes that are happening in the technology industry as they may have a broad impact on our lives.

Data Speaks: Why Some Companies Succeed and Others Collapse

Yahoo! Endemic Ordeals

In the summer of 2017, Verizon completed the acquisition of Yahoo (core business) for $4.48 billion,[35] (as reported by the *Washington Post*). A flash back to 2008, Microsoft proposed to acquire the company for over $44 billion; Yahoo rejected the offer. The company was once valued at over $125 billion according to the *New York Times*[36] and the *Wall Street Journal.*[37] Over the years, Yahoo bought over 100 companies, most of them failed or became ultimately unproductive. Something was fundamentally wrong and was never corrected. We can also assume that Yahoo never looked backwards to assess its unsuccessful acquisitions.

The company consistently overlooked its data and over the years, Yahoo has always been on par with Google and Facebook as it relates to unique visitors. Instead of using the data generated from the site to gain insight on where the customers found value, the company maintained the same philosophy of acquiring and attempting to take on almost everything. Yahoo missed countless opportunities to make an assessment that would consist of analyzing the behavior and geo-locations of their users as well as the times spent in specific areas of the platform. This would have in turn created a pathway to foresee market shifts by using its own data to innovate and explore new businesses. This would most likely have been a better bet. It is hard to assess whether Yahoo's many acquisitions were informed by data, or strong use cases or simply by a culture of business impulses. In 2013, Yahoo acquired a startup company called Summly—an application built by a bright 17-year-old high school student—for $30 million, then dropped it into a black hole. Evidently, this was not a data-driven decision because its implementation did not have a clear use case and ultimately, did not work out. Data is not the panacea for all business decisions, but the organizations that make it an integral part of their decision-making processes will continue to lead the way.

To this point, Yahoo is still alive and remains a popular multi-platform technology company. In 2017, it became part of a consortium of brands named Oath (a subsidiary of Verizon), along with AOL, and other companies. Hopefully, Verizon will learn and will eventually compel Yahoo to finally find its identity and position itself for the future. Regardless, Yahoo is still attracting a high volume of users and generating data that can turn the company into a lucrative business, content, weather or health data hub. Doing so would help Verizon turn their acquisition into a data maven initiative—assuming they will adopt systematic approaches (as discussed in chapter 10) to value, prioritize and protect the privacy of their users. The next step will define where the acquisition is heading—toward redemption or the graveyard.

Google's Game Changing Playbook

Google and its parent company Alphabet made a fair share of acquisitions too, but they managed to build one of the world's most valuable companies, now a behemoth that seems unstoppable. At the core of the difference is how Google has bet on data and analytics to inform its decision-making process. Yahoo chased too many misfit priorities as a runaway buyer. It passively bet on a future that was not dictated by relevant, accurate and reliable data. Google has made data and analytics the spine of its core business, and offers big data and analytics solutions that permits its users to "capture, process, store and analyze data."[38]

YouTube

All of Google's attempts in social media have been unsuccessful. The purchase of YouTube in 2006 put Google at the top echelon of social media networks. The platform bought billions in ad revenue and created a market for influencers to build their own channels. YouTube has become the world's premier video search engine with social features and an easy way to embed its content on any site. Keeping YouTube as a stand-alone company should be celebrated as one of Google's greatest business decisions. This revealed a playbook that may be overlooked, but has demonstrated how to manage the post acquisitions of technology companies. YouTube taps into the tech giant ecosystem, smart algorithms and in return, it gives Google direct access to massive quantities of streaming content in hundreds of languages. We can request music through YouTube with a simple voice command. Imagine YouTube's ability to gather and store the voice data of users across the globe by requesting or ordering for example, their favorites songs or movies in French, Spanish, Arabic, Vietnamese, Russian, Swahili, German, Italian, Haitian Creole or Portuguese. All of these languages in addition to widely distinct English accents or pronunciations through speech navigation, and videos uploaded on a daily basis on the platform. The variety of speeches combined with the high volume of widely available unstructured data (voice, text and video), could be curated to serve as vital datasets to train and feed AI systems—assuming the company follows a rigorous data protection and privacy protocol. Amazingly, we have made significant progress, but we are still a long way from developing a highly efficient natural language processing (NLP) technology with the ability to tap into most of the languages used on social media platforms such as YouTube. Having the systems to facilitate direct interaction as well as collecting and mining big data in compliance to data privacy, constitutes a fundamental step forward for the tech giant as voice technology becomes more and more prevalent in our culture, homes and habits.

Waze

Waze is a community-based traffic and navigation app. This acquisition demonstrates how Google connected the dots and used foresight to make one of its most consequential decisions. The early stage startup was up and coming, and presented a potential challenge to Google Maps. Google eventually bought Waze in 2013, but did not combine it with Google Maps. Waze remains unique and continues to build on innovation as a community-based data sourcing navigation system. We can argue that the dots were indeed connected to understand that with a completely different use case, culture and DNA, Waze would not merge well with Google Maps.

Despite not being merged, both companies are still thriving and as a result, Google is better off—they do not have to consider Waze as a competitor.

Waze's acquisition served multiple purposes; it allowed Google to maintain its leadership in the space and also kept a potential competitor at bay. Ultimately, it brought a strong community with a wealth of data that Google could tap into to shape its future with autonomous vehicle technology or interconnected systems for example. Combined with the data and analytics of Google Maps, the company is well positioned in self-driving car technology and can help smart cities make more effective and efficient planning decisions. This proves that acquisitions must live well beyond their intended value.

Google has made a few bad acquisitions as well, but taking into consideration where the company is, they have clearly learned from those failed experiments. By connecting the dots, you can detect patterns, and use insight to avoid repeating the same mistakes. Thus, despite some unsuccessful and costly deals such as Motorola, Google's acquisitions and mergers have not impeded the company's progress. Some of Google's purchases seem to go deep into foresights that few could see or imagine—betting on data brings a level of mystique that makes the company (almost) untouchable. Consider for a moment, the significance of the Android operating system (purchased in 2005), a seemingly quiet deal as few could imagine how Android would rule in the digital age. The value that it brought by taking Google to the world's communications arena can never be quantified. What is indeed notable is Google's parent company, Alphabet, was reported to be worth well over $600 billion in 2017, and is on course to a $1 trillion market value according to *Fortune*.[39]

Facebook's Way

Facebook seems to have mastered how to use data and analytics to iterate, navigate and build strong partnerships with its acquisitions while allowing them to continue operating independently. The purchase of WhatsApp and Instagram positioned the company as a preeminent global leader that is deeply woven into the social fabric of cultures, digital interactions and relationships across the globe. This remarkable and complex venture presents both challenges and opportunities for the world's gateway of social networking and communications. I will discuss more about Facebook in subsequent chapters.

Reflection

The practical questions and assessments that senior executives must consider are whether, when, and to what extent are new entries likely to occur given the growth of digital transformation and the rising trend of automating key segments of varied industries. They must also determine when to acquire a potential competitor and particularly how to manage and decide the type of integration to be implemented.

The New Era of Business: Data and Analytics–Digital Strategies

To begin with, let us consider Whole Foods, a prime example in the grocery retail industry. It failed to capitalize on the impact of digital transformation as its competitive advantage shifted, and its core business (organic products) became mainstream. We can also take a subsequent look at how Amazon consumes the e-commerce industry, and how to take advantage of inefficiencies in the market as well as the natural disruption in the automotive and transportation industry with Tesla. Then, there is Apple. According to its CEO, Tim Cook, the company makes data privacy an integral part of the design of its products. In the following sections, I will explore these cases and the benefit of connecting the dots as a personal choice to advance your career.

Whole Foods: Lost Sight and Saved by Amazon

In August 2017, Amazon, the e-commerce giant, purchased Whole Foods for $13.7 billion. Founded in 1980, the Whole Foods supermarket chain built its brand on natural/organic products and foods without artificial preservatives when other companies had no interest in servicing this segment of the market. It attracted a legion of strong and loyal shoppers and became an important player in the industry as a result. One can make the argument that Whole Foods connected the dots to address the needs of a growing consumer base and emerged as a market leader. It became the go-to store for customers who wanted to feel that they were purchasing and consuming healthy food. As years went by, more players began to enter the market with similar products. Initially, the competition consisted of just a few outliers, but soon selling natural and organic foods became the trend in grocery shopping. Mainstream chains eventually offered their own in-house (and much less expensive), organic lines. Ultimately, Whole Foods no longer had a competitive advantage because customers could purchase similar products more affordably almost everywhere—even online. Online grocery shopping quickly became a more ubiquitous reality.

The company began to struggle to find new answers in order to remain competitive. Adopting a hybrid model that would combine an integrated digital shopping and delivery system with their in-store experience could have given them another head start in the market in the digital era. Whole Foods did not predict the shift quickly enough and was late in adapting to the digital trend of online grocery shopping. The company's revenue began to decline—then lost its mojo as stock prices plunged. It was then that Amazon made the informed decision to purchase the brand.

Amazon: The King of Digital Commerce

It is nearly impossible to talk about corporate success and the efficient use of data without mentioning Amazon. This is a company that uses data and analytics to identify inefficiencies in the market and takes advantage of those who failed to foresee their shortcomings. Amazon has managed to build an empire by touching varied points in our lives as a data-driven company that pays attention to the details that other enterprises tend to overlook. It masters the art of instant recommendations through the efficient use of machine learning—the company knows our purchasing habits and interests at the first click or swipe. It collects and analyzes data ranging from telephone support hold times, to how shelves are stocked, to transportation systems, and delivery times in real-time—all with a constant focus on maximizing efficiency.

The Disruptor's Secret: A Cursory Look into Mobility

Taking advantage of inefficiencies could be a secret ingredient or a powerful guiding principle for disruptions. We see similar patterns played across varied industries and beyond. The next short case study explores how Tesla Motors has transformed the automotive Industry.

Tesla Pioneered the New Age of Transportation

Tesla Motors generated a trend in electric vehicles (EVs) but began as an outlier when very few believed that they would be able to pull it off. Currently, nearly all traditional automakers, in addition to a host of startup companies across the globe have started making electric and autonomous vehicles in order to remain competitive. As a pioneer, Tesla transformed the mobility market, and EVs have now become the pattern in the automotive industry. Disruptors are often risk takers who are rewarded. As of April 2017, Tesla was reportedly worth over $55 billion. They surpassed traditional car companies (General Motors and Ford) to "Become the most valuable U.S. carmaker."[40] An amazing feat if considered that the company was just an outlier just few years ago. In 2017, Tesla entered the Fortune 500 companies list, moved up from 588 to 383—and ranked 260 in 2018 (up 123 spots), according to Fortune 500.[41] The company also produced advanced solar panel and battery technology. Tesla's treasure trove is its car data-enabled capabilities (mapping, driving behaviors, videos, etc.). Tesla is becoming a data powerhouse,[42] with a commanding lead in how it uses and crowdsources data in real-time from its worldwide fleet of vehicles that are on the road. I assume that the company follows the best practices to ask and receive consent from its customers, and that data privacy features are built-in and embedded into their system. A 2016, McKinsey report entitled "*Monetizing Car Data*" estimates that the potential value opportunity from car data could reach between $450 to $750 billion by 2030.[43]

Apple: Leading in the Valley

Apple is at the top of every metrics system that explores how successful enterprises use data to build customer engagement that is almost cult like. The company has gone to unimaginable lengths since its inception to protect the data of their customers. They understand that their future depends on it. This seems an integral part of the company in a world where privacy is just a hack away from spilling all over the web. Apple clearly knows that data privacy could become the one challenge that could disrupt powerful enterprises. As a result, they conceive, design and build their products accordingly. Tim Cook, the CEO of Apple, said during an interview with Laurie Segall on CNN Business, "Privacy is a fundamental human right," and added "It is one of these key civil liberties that define what it is to be an American…it has been under attack."[44] He also indicated that pointing fingers at other companies would not be a viable way to address this issue and reflected on how "To make the web an unbelievable place not only for ourselves, but more importantly for the kids that are on it."[45] Apple's foresight to remain ahead of this challenge is commendable and customers will remain loyal to the brand until they prove otherwise. The company's unmatched forward-thinking, user privacy approach and exceptional designs has truly transformed our lives. As a result, Apple is already one of the world's most valuable and impactful companies in the history of humankind. The brand will continue to lead the way until it has lost the ability to make special and unique products.

To be clear, as I conclude this section, every single company (with no exception), collects, stores and processes the data of their users or customers. Some perform the task in a more aggressive manner than others and we may never know the extent as most of the collection is executed without consent. This action creates serious privacy concerns and security risks.

It's Personal: Connecting the Dots to Advance Your Career

Occasionally, the ability to connect the dots is beneficial as a personal choice and lessons can also be learnt to inform a broader business goal.

Stay Relevant: As another quick example, consider the fact that the subscription business model is a fast and emerging trend that will change how a sales team operates. If you are a sales manager, it is important to assess how this trend can impact your career and how you can position yourself and your team to remain relevant to the future of your business.

To the C-Suite: Is there an ultimate path to the top in corporations? Assuming that all the conditions are met, you have done all the right things to advance your career, but for some reason you feel plateaued or are stuck in a mid-level management labyrinth. You have a sponsor that advocates on your behalf as well as great mentors. You also have the results to show that you are worthy of the C-Suite—yet you cannot penetrate the ceiling. Many things can explain the reason behind your condition. However, as you progress it is essential to have a clear picture of your situation. The ultimate question is how many people with the same conditions succeeded and made it to the C-suite? That is a backward reflection. Now, look forward—is the same path in the golden age of data and analytics driven by artificial intelligence still valid? Considering the present condition, would those who made it repeat the same feat? Again, it is imperative to put aside traditional barriers that keep women and minorities plateaued at the mid-level management. Evidently, there is a lot more than just being on the right path to reach the C-suite.

The point here is, connecting the dots backward is the first step. Next, look forward by assessing career trends, outliers and patterns that can provide meaningful insight as to how you can advance your career. This may require the need to improve your skillset, rebrand or pivot and change your path accordingly. These steps will not guarantee that you will make it, but if that is your goal, then place yourself in a better position to get there.

Reflection

Let's explore the following questions and determine how you fit:

1. What are the personal challenges in adopting data and analytics in your business practices?
2. Are there current training initiatives and incentives available in your organization to help you develop data and analytics skills?
3. Do you know how and where to access the data that is relevant to your roles?
4. Are you confidently able to communicate your business needs to, and collaborate with IT, data scientists, and data analytics specialists?
5. How do other managers in your organization approach data and analytics?
6. If you have used data and analytics in your roles, have you had some success stories?

Can you think of two instances over the past three reporting cycles where you felt that having the knowledge of data and analytics would have made you better able to share your stories?

Managers: Ready. Set. Go!

The TOP techniques introduced in chapter 2 consist of simple actions that could make data and analytics work for you and they are essential for managers to assess. They can help uncover some relevant findings to act on or create new use cases that will position the brand, service, product, or organization to ensure a strong analytical knowledge base. More importantly, managers who value these codes will have a competitive edge and will add value while contributing to the growth of their organization. What would happen if they do not? Well, they might need to start paying attention to the headlines surrounding failing companies or the imminent shift in the workforce over the next few years.

The next step will be what you do with the insights as a manager. How will you use what you know and discover? After a manager is able to detect important trends, outliers and patterns, they are able to share the information with the data and analytics team to leverage their insights and develop models. The manager can use the findings to drill down and investigate other attributes and discover more relevant insights. Being the first to identify a trend that generates actionable insights in your business can catapult your career, secure a comfortable seat at the table and even help you land in the C-Suite.

The key point to takeaway here is that you can observe the world around you and focus on what seems routine or unusual—this could refer to health care devices, talent strategies, or simply a product that you use every day. Next, be curious as you determine whether or not something is missing. Identify inefficiencies—if you pick the right device, service or products, the chances are you could transform your company, division or an entire industry. Simply put, what you may find by being observant and analytical could play a vital role in your next business endeavor.

4

The Four Stages of Analytics

"Intelligence is the ability to adapt to change."
—Stephen Hawking

Descriptive - Diagnostic - Predictive - Prescriptive Analytics

This is the future. The ability to understand the impact of emerging technology on data collection and advanced analytics methods will transform your organization and define your career in this 21st century. With the exponential growth in computing power, automation, AI taking over tasks usually performed by humans, in addition to keeping up with the rapid increase in the volume of data currently available becomes more challenging every day. Automation is impacting everything, particularly how we analyze data. This process has been rapidly evolving and has already reached impressive advances that seemed unattainable just a few years ago. Companies are armed with technology that has the potential to unearth insights from the past and the present as well as projecting into the future. Deploying the right solutions that combine human and machine intelligence remains a constant challenge. This is necessary to help organizations uncover insights that inform operational and strategic business decisions and gain competitive advantages. The *how* takes us to what is described as stages of analytics.

Analytics Lifecycle: Continuous Loop

As we move forward, it is important to keep in mind that projections will deviate from the models as unforeseen events occur. A well-designed and advanced analytics system will adjust and recalibrate the models to help you stay on course and continue moving you forward. Certainly, the four stages of analytics (descriptive, diagnostic, predictive, and prescriptive), have largely been discussed by varied organizations (Gartner, McKinsey, Deloitte, Cisco, IBM, Accenture), with different iterations and models. Determining their fundamental applications or values for business operations remains elusive as there are limited real-life examples for a manager or an executive to grasp and process how exactly these stages apply. This text will provide a more practical and simplified approach in demonstrating how they have already been incorporated in our everyday routines. It becomes essential therefore, to understand the four stages or cornerstones of analytics in order to remain viable, adapt, increase ROI, work faster and smarter and be able to unearth insights from your data in real-time.

The four stages of analytics offer an opportunity to conduct data analysis from the **baseline** level before advancing to the in-depth exploration and interpretation of each stage. This approach also helps guide and establish an agile relationship as to how the four phases of analytics work together at specific stages of the analytics processes to gain real-time actionable insights. They are essential in helping to understand how advanced **data analysis** evolves in time and space. They also aid in identifying what forms of analytics are important at different stages of the evolution **process** to gain timely intelligence.

These four (4) types of analytics can be performed in connection to the TOP techniques as previously discussed in chapter 2. A Gartner's model[46] (2014) offers a well-organized and comprehensive way to conceptualize the four types of advanced analytics. Below is an iteration of the model to explain my case and subsequent illustrations.

Four Stages of Analytics

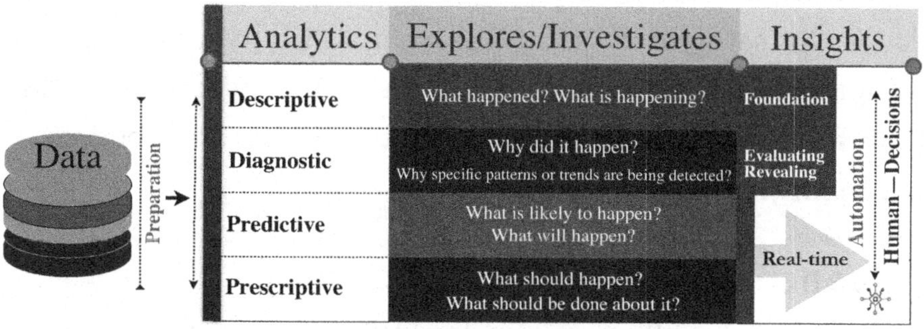

Sources: Gartner, IBM, McKinsey, Cisco, Accenture

The model shown above flows from descriptive, diagnostic, predictive and prescriptive analytics. These are the four fundamental stages of analytics that are largely consistent with what has been previously documented, reported, adopted, and described by varied reputable organizations such as Gartner, Accenture, Oracle and IBM to name a few.

Below, I explore the lifecycle, from their evolution to applications. In order to address this in further detail, I discuss how they apply during a short driving trip using the navigation system (Waze) as a case study. First, let's take a cursory look into the definition of the four stages of analytics to put our discussion into context. I share more in-depth definitions at the end of the chapter and the case study provides real-life examples to understand their applications—this is often missing in the discussions.

Descriptive: What happened? It provides insights into the past.

Diagnostic: Why did it happen and why are specific patterns or trends being detected?

Predictive: What is likely to happen? Or what will happen? It helps forecast, and is probabilistic in nature. It sets the direction.

Prescriptive: What should happen? It helps to make recommendations in real-time. This can be accomplished by using cognitive computing systems. It helps you navigate the complex direction to your destination and remain in control during those periods of uncertainty.

Advanced Analytics: It's a Journey

These four pillars are vital and fundamental in ensuring that your business is successful during transformative times. There is more depth to them than appears at first glance. Though not a rigorous requirement, you can apply them as a sequential loop—beginning first with descriptive analytics as your baseline to assess what happened and what is happening in your enterprise. Then proceed with a diagnostic to understand why specific trends, outliers or patterns are being detected. Decisions are made and consequently, companies succeed or fail based upon their ability to strategically use these techniques. By ignoring for example, the ability to assess "what is happening and why it happened", a business will most likely be vulnerable to disruption. Such organizations will be ill-equipped in applying predictive analytics to forecast future outcomes or in making contingency plans, identifying blind spots and adopting initiatives to unlock hidden values. These steps are essential for predictive analytics in helping to uncover and map out what should happen, and in prescribing in real-time which strategies to adopt as you move forward. Let us explore how they will actually apply and hold true through real-life examples.

Why They Matter?

Driving from point A to point B—you will probably ask: what does analytics have to do with it? In the following case study, I illustrate and simplify in a digestible and navigable form the four stages of data and analytics. Let us consider my routine commute from Fairfax, VA (A) to Silver Spring or Bethesda, MD (B) for example, in order to explain these four concepts and solve the equation of moving from point A to point B.

The story in this case is adjusted, adapted and only used for learning purposes and to explain these very complex concepts of advanced analytics. The purpose is to use an everyday experience like driving to help you improve your advanced analytics capacity. Understanding them will lead to great productivity and operational efficiency for your career and your organization.

Real World Application of the Four Stages of Analytics

Case Study set-up

I spend quite some time in traffic during my daily commute. On average, I waste about 1 hour and 20 minutes per week during an approximately 6-hour drive in the DMV area (D.C., Maryland, and Virginia), to and from my office or meetings. According to INRIX Research traffic data, Washington, D.C. is the 6th most congested city in the United States—with an average congestion rate of 11 percent and costing the city over $6 billion in 2017. The INRIX Research estimates the total cost of traffic congestion in the United States at over $300 billion. Additionally, 10 of the top 25 most congested cities in the world are located in the U.S. from the 2017 ranking of 1,360 cities.[47] Traffic congestion is a constant global issue. As a result of frequent traffic congestion in the DMV area, I am always trying to find ways to shorten my commute through the Waze app.

Traffic congestion is a perfect case scenario to explain advanced analytics. Similar to analytics, it can be unpredictable at times and difficult to navigate. In the DMV area, the congestion on highways and city roads can be extremely frustrating during peak commuting hours to the point that access to the **E-Z Pass** lanes can fluctuate from $1 to over $25 on the same route depending on the flow of traffic. From this perspective over the past three years, I have developed the habit of turning on my Waze app before beginning each trip. This pattern helps me predict my ETAs and potential situations that could cause severe delays. In addition, I tend to read the electronic boards displaying toll costs to access the express way from Virginia to Maryland and vice versa. This strategy tends to serve as a predictor for traffic congestion as the price varies accordingly. What do all of these details have to do with the four stages of analytics? A lot more than you might imagine! The first lesson to be learned here is to always try to stay connected and informed. Let us navigate what this actually entails. So, let us begin.

The Case

It was around 9:15 am on a Thursday morning and I was driving to downtown Silver Spring, MD from Fairfax, VA. I opened my Waze and entered my destination. Waze is a community-based traffic and navigation system app used by over 100 million global active users.[48] The app uses geolocation data from its network of users, which in turn creates a culture of community-based driver engagement where millions are sharing data on road closures, work zones, speed traps, accidents and traffic congestion in real-time every day.

Insights from Behind the Scene

Before I proceed with the demonstration, it is important to understand what happens in the kitchen or behind the scenes. Waze demonstrates what Thomas W. Malone describes in his book *Superminds*[49] as the power of people and machines thinking and working together. Waze, to some extent, represents a useful application of this philosophy: the power of a group of people and computers acting together. I rely on this vision of the future to explain the four stages of analytics. Waze models the real-time data from millions of users, combined with advanced cognitive technology to inform other drivers on road conditions such as traffic congestion and unexpected diversions or delays. It helps commuters find the most efficient routes in real-time based on its recommendations, thus "outsmarting" traffic. Keep in mind that if a driver during this particular process is familiar with or has experienced living or working in the area, she would be using her critical judgment to decide on the best routes to take rather than completely relying on the app. When applied to business operations, you have to become well acclimated with your industry and organization's data in order to know when to use your judgment. You cannot and should not ever outsource your judgment to the machine.

Given the complexity of advanced analytics, chances are your organization may not have a comprehensive data strategy and ecosystem to facilitate end-to-end analytics solutions in its business operation. I explain how to collect the data in several chapters of the book in methods that range from traditional to automation. At this stage, let us consider the 2 key points to follow as you prepare for the symbiotic relationship[50] (humans + machines) with your data and analytics projects. *First,* it is critical to focus on the value of human judgment—it matters. Analytics as presented in this book is not a swap, push button or voice command solution. This is vital to understand in order to exercise and value critical thinking, intuition, creativity, ethics and moral judgment in the decision-making process. *Secondly,* consider unforeseen events, such as a *cas de force majeure* beyond your control that could disrupt your journey—thus the need to develop an integrated system. Analytics is not a constant or a continuous line, it fluctuates and is likely to be influenced by a series of factors based on the three codes (TOP Techniques) which are previously described in chapter 2—namely trends, outliers and patterns. By nature, humans are ill-prepared to deal with the unknown and machines are designed to handle things that are better related to precision, repetitive tasks, high powered computation, pattern recognition and reaction time. There is one thing you can be sure of; an outlier or event will emerge with risk to disrupt your journey. With that in mind, reflect on this: the unpredictable is not the biggest challenge to your enterprise, it will happen that is a given—your inability to adjust in real-time however, is actually your biggest threat. The role of an efficient analytics model is to reflect on the real world, which is marred in complexity. With that said, let us get back to the road.

"Every Once in a while, a revolutionary product comes along that changes everything." – Steve Jobs

Navigating the Unknown

As I departed, Waze indicated that the road was clear with an ETA of approximately 30 minutes for an approximate 20-mile commute. Relief of the possible short drive, I closed the app and listened to my routine Podcasts. From route 66 E, the drive was a smooth ride to the 64B exit towards I-495 N. About 2 miles on I-495 N, I noticed that traffic was slowing down and soon realized it was due to an unforeseen event that the navigation system could not or did not predict. I then looked at the board posted on the side of the road which indicated that there was a crash and that the left shoulder was blocked. Road accidents remain generally unpredictable—during the journey to your destination, things will change and what is really vital is how you adjust to these changes. Even outside of small probabilities, uncertainties are always present on the road. This analogy is similar to any business venture. Put your resources on developing and testing systems that will adapt to change and adjust in real-time—this will work as Waze does to instantly suggest new options when an event occurs. This could be any number of things in business—a new disruptive entrant, a breakdown in your system, a reliable partner suddenly defaulting, or there could be some kind of outbreak or natural disaster. Some will come with higher risks than others, but they *will* come. As a result, I want to reiterate that you must build systems to adjust and adapt to changes. This is the essence of this chapter and subsequent ones. Advanced analytics offers real-time recommendations for course correction because the unknown is part of the real world—a constant that you must address and handle along the journey.

The descriptive information that was posted on the traffic board was important, but it did not offer much besides what had happened (a car crash). As a result, I went back on the navigation app to seek insights as to what was happening in real-time in order to update my ETA and find solutions that would enable me to avoid further traffic congestion. AI and Machine Learning powered systems (such as Waze) have the ability to learn from past events and assess consequences. They can also build models and act to predict new outcomes in **real-time**. There as you see it, begins the journey from descriptive to prescriptive analytics.

The analytical and power of Waze to adjust in real-time and deliver solutions provides a tested and sustained form of technology that demonstrates the stages of analytics. This offers a revolutionary way to pair humans and machines for intuitive and cognitive collaboration. This partnership is described in a 2017 Deloitte article, entitled *Cognitive collaboration: Why humans and computers think better together.* The authors suggest that we "view machine and human intelligence as complementary, with each bringing its own strengths to the table."[51] The story below demonstrates the application of advanced analytics, and machine learning technologies to support human efforts.

Augmented Intelligence: Human-machine Symbiotic Collaboration

Waze informed me of a crash (what happened), and gave me the specific spot and distance from my current location near exit 45 (**Descriptive**). As in every crash, emergency medical services are generally called and present at the scene to assess needs and provide care while police officers are present to record what happened and why it happened and act accordingly (**Diagnostic**). Waze showed a visual map of the road (overview of the landscape), and displayed a sidebar to indicate the expected time in traffic from red to yellow. It was estimated at approximately 15 minutes from my location and it updated my ETA in real-time—I could also visualize what would happen, so I could act accordingly (**Predictive**). Subsequently, I clicked on the route options from the app to get recommendations of possible alternative routes. Waze provided (3) possibilities with great visual detail of what should happen (recommended routes in real-time) and what to expect based on each selection (**Prescriptive**). Being well informed, I made a judgment call by using my intuition and knowledge of the area and evaluated the time (duration) and distance (miles) of the recommended routes (insights) to make the best decision. As a result of being familiar with the routes—which seemed fairly obvious, there was no guarantee that I would be there any faster as other events might occur along the way. I made an informed decision that by deciding to take the next exit as one of the options would not change my new ETA significantly, so I stayed put. Consequently,

I sent a voice note to my colleague to let her know that I would be few minutes late for our routine meeting. I managed to switch from the left lane as the app also indicated that it was closed ahead, and I stayed on course to my destination (decision) and shaved a few minutes of my travel time. The important message here is to always keep in mind that while conducting data analysis, you will still have to make the decisions, but they should be informed first by using the data, intuition, your judgment, then experience to draw the right conclusion.

During my drive from Fairfax, VA, I was not in the position to investigate the factors as to why or how the crash happened. The details surrounding that situation would only be available in a report recorded by the police officers who first responded to the scene of the crash. They would make the determination as to who was at fault, issue tickets if necessary, then document, and write the report. The insurance companies of the parties involved would then need the diagnostic information to determine how to proceed with their claim decisions.

Analytics Works Best When Machines Are Used to Make People Think Smarter

As I proceeded on I-495 N, nearly 12 minutes later, I found that the road was finally decongested because a tow truck had arrived to move the cars from the scene of the accident to ease the flow of the traffic. I continued towards my destination and kept Waze on. I decided to exit on 36 towards Bethesda and Rockville, Maryland, as it seemed there was slow traffic on I-495 W towards the downtown Silver Spring exit (31B). Upon exiting, I followed Waze since I was unfamiliar with that specific area and remained on high alert. I also like to use the navigation system to detect the speed limit which is sometimes hard to determine and to avoid speed traps on the road that are more common in Maryland. Waze led me to a comfortable and more familiar area near Old Georgetown in Bethesda, MD. I felt at ease, and proceeded to my destination.

As I was driving towards my destination that day, Waze showed my current speed in red as soon as I exceeded it even by 1 mph. In my case, I reduced my speed from 45 to about 36 mph. The signs for speed limits on the road are conceived and intended to reinforce safety, and Waze make it seamless.

Absence of Guidance: The Drive to Nowhere

Further down the road, I noticed a few other cars had slowed down, and a driver sped to beyond 45 mph only to be stopped at the next light. I drove slowly on the lane right next to him and kept my head straight. This supports the notion that driving at a safer speed does not necessarily make your trip shorter,[52] particularly in an urban area. The driver was probably unaware that the driving speed had changed from 45 to 35 mph, or he may have simply chosen to ignore it. In some cases, there could be a speed trap set specifically to catch unsafe drivers. Unfortunately, this speeding diver could have caused yet another accident, and would more than likely receive a ticket if there were speeding cameras. Waze's speed limit comparison in real-time if taken into consideration, helps keep drivers in check and aware of their speed, which is an important factor to observing road safety. Similarly, a well-designed analytics system should do the same for your business. It is up to you to move at the right speed, know when to accelerate and particularly when to slow down.

The Backup Plan

The navigation system in my car is not as advanced as Waze, but it is always available when Waze has No GPS signal. It sends me warning messages such as road constructions ahead and keeps me on track as I navigate through the tunnels. Additionally, it remains reliable in case the app navigation system falters due to low cell phone signals or other issues. Do you have a backup system if or when your sophisticated analytics system fails? This is important to consider and to avoid getting lost in your business journey. If executed correctly, you will more than likely reach your desired destination safely and remain in control as you adjust when necessary.

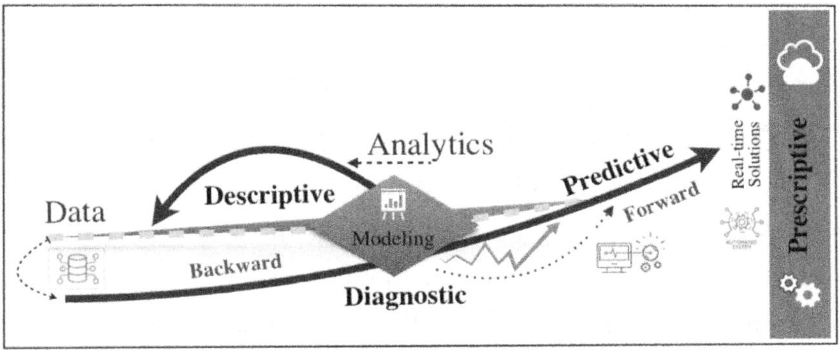

Sources: Informed by various publications
(including Gartner, McKinsey, Accenture, IBM, Oracle, Cisco)

A Deep Dive

Descriptive analytics – which refers to what happened (a look into the rearview mirror)—is an important part of the data analysis process. This can be used to detect trends, identify outliers and discover patterns. The term "descriptive analytics" is employed to detect what happened and could help assess what types of opportunities or challenges are hidden in your data. Using the right metrics can help prepare for the unknown and assess the measurable impact of a decision on your business. Descriptive serves as the simple idea of starting with what is known to birth new opportunities.

"Descriptive Analytics is the examination of data or content, usually manually performed, to answer the question "What happened?" (or What is happening?), characterized by traditional business intelligence (BI) and visualizations such as pie charts, bar charts, line graphs, tables, or generated narratives."[53] – Gartner

"... In simple terms, descriptive analytics examine a company's data and past performance to find the reasons behind past successes or failures."[54] – Accenture

Diagnostic analytics can be considered as a deep plunge into the data to understand for example, the factors that drive an outlier or why the event happened. Simply put, it would serve as the question, "*Why you didn't see this coming?*" Let us say that during your analysis, you notice discrepancies or detect outliers in the data. It is your responsibility to explain what happened and describe the why. Diagnostic analytics is important to investigate and address inconsistency and question the reliability of data. An outlier could be the beginning of an emerging trend, a security breach or a serious problem that requires immediate action to avoid potential disruption. The findings can turn out to be invaluable. Consider the case of Whole Foods, the company ignored when other stores entered its market and delayed adjusting to digital transformation despite its savvy customer base. The outliers became the trend in the market and as a result it lost a significant share of the market to traditional grocery stores offering the same products at lower prices. I discussed this in great detail in chapter 3; *Connecting the Dots.*

Diagnostic analytics provides tentative and exploratory insights into the how and why of trends, outliers and patterns that are formed over time and findings that can be utilized to mitigate or take advantage of their potential effects on your organization. Further, diagnostics analytics can be used to build models to help guide where you should explore, where challenges may be emerging and how to look for deeper insights. It can help you understand the dynamics of the market and to explore how these indicators have changed. In return, you will be able to synchronize the predictive impact of data on the organization's long-term viability.

Predictive analytics is at the crossroads of what is known and looks beyond what is possible to inform you about what is likely coming. It helps you stay on track during times of uncertainty. This stage connects the dots backwards, by using past performances to reach predictable success and forecast future outcomes. As Accenture puts it: "Predictive analytics come in several forms. The first is **statistical analysis,** which tries to determine why something is happening by searching for patterns and trends in the data. **Forecasting/extrapolation** examines the data to determine what will happen in the future. **Predictive modeling** explores what will happen next, given past patterns and future plans. **Optimization** looks at the data and tries to determine what can be altered or tweaked to advance the best possible outcome."[55] – Accenture

Prescriptive analytics is where cognitive computing excels to augment and enhance human abilities beyond what is known and predictable. It helps identify the blind-spots and offers multifaceted benefits to improve decision-making. Additionally, it adjusts and adapts in real-time. It is not always guaranteed that you will succeed without a potential risk of disruption. In the next chapter, I elaborate on why it is so imperative to build efficient and adjustable analytics systems. Your business can and will be impacted by unforeseen events beyond your control and/or cas de force majeure such as wars, natural disasters, or other types of situations as previously described. However, as the event occurs, new information emerges, and the system will adjust and use the real-time data to inform what you should do next. No matter what happens, by betting on prescriptive analytics, you will have new insights to act upon as the world spins.

5

Advanced Analytics: Steering Through Unmapped Territories

"Contrary to the past when various companies failed due to the delay in adopting technology, the future's disruption might come from underrating humans, overusing robots and failing to build a symbiotic workforce (humans + machines) for the future."

—Journel Joseph

Are you unsure of how to prepare for the road ahead? How to manage or navigate through cloudy roads under timely pressure? Uncertain of the right turn to take? Leading a business operation, or running a government department can draw close comparisons to driving to some extent. However, when the navigation system fails to deliver due to a low signal or it disconnects unexpectedly, what do you do? When shareholders, analysts and the media already proclaim that you are doomed for failure, what is your next course of action? I call this the *gut zone*. In this chapter, I share a few cases of when leaders from companies such as Domino's, Netflix, Merck, CVS Health and Microsoft had to make gutsy decisions that could potentially have put everything at risk. As it turns out, these same decisions are the very reasons why they are in their current positions. Analytics is similar to a navigation system—it serves as a reliable tool that keeps you informed in real-time and helps you steer through potentially unmapped territories to arrive safely at your destination.

The AI-powered analytics system is changing the conversation with its ability to adjust as fast as unforeseen events happen and can actually offer in real-time renewed alternatives where your forecast previously failed. Ultimately, you need the four stages of analytics (as discussed in chapter 4), to ensure that you secure dependable choices to effectively tackle difficult and unpredictable events. These steps are necessary in handling the complex decisions that are made on a day-to-day basis. Being informed to make the right judgement call in every turn will save lives, time, and money or even keep your organization from falling into painful or disruptive situations. Case in point, Waze has wide-ranging features that I used to illustrate the four stages of analytics. It is also important to remember that as with all technology—Waze has its flaws and limits, so the final decision would have to be yours. The point here is that data and analytics can help you avoid reckless driving, or awful decisions as well as provide you with valuable insights to ensure that your company gains competitive advantages. It enables you to remain in control of the speed of any turbulence or shift in the market as well as permitting you to prevail when the world seems to spin out of control.

It's All About Real-time Adjustment: Plain and Simple

The car crash as indicated in the previous chapter added approximately 12 minutes to my commute on that Thursday morning. Though I did not anticipate this detour during my trip, I was able to adjust accordingly as it occurred. I made it to my destination later than the original ETA, but I was informed and in control of my driving. The Waze app also has a feature that provides information regarding different parking lots within walking distance of my destination which is based on the address initially entered in the app. Upon entering the parking garage, I read the signs prompting me about available parking spots on each floor through means of the sensor data in free and occupied lots. Shortly after, I proceeded, parked and walked to my meeting. The Waze navigation system presents the most intriguing way to measure how advanced analytics could fare in the real world. Throughout the course of my journey, the app efficiently scanned the road down to the smallest parts, such as potholes, then mined through large amounts of geolocation data sharing from drivers to tangling the range from very basic to the overall big picture. It does all of this while delivering real-time insights.

The 4 stages of analytics are becoming essential for business and are also moving at a pace that has transformed how enterprises operate in addition to how they address considerable uncertainty due to talent gaps across almost all industries. Options such as Waze seemed intangible just a few years ago, yet today, I tend to take it for granted. It seems hard to remember the days when I had to use MapQuest, print my itinerary and search for street names (while driving) that sometimes did not exist or had been removed. By using a printed map, I was not able to read the street names in unfamiliar neighborhoods. I would wind up turning around until I was able to figure it out. Similarly, many companies are still stuck in the printed MapQuest era to guide them through their destination in the digital age. They are not prepared for the fast changing business landscape, and have not moved beyond the classic data and analytics model. They are running behind and are outdated by using unfit strategies to confront modern day problems. Quite frankly, some have lost their way while others are speeding out of control and are unable to catch up. By functioning in this manner, it is only a matter of time before they become defunct due to their inability to adapt and innovate. Waze helped me understand what happened and forecasted the road ahead while suggesting actions to help me envision the potential outcomes in advance. I acted on the insights to stay in control of the journey from Fairfax, VA to my final destination. Personally, this process has become a pattern that I repeat on a daily basis. Similarly, in business it is important to remain informed and ready to take on unforeseen challenges on the tough roads ahead.

Go Later–Go Now

An interesting feature that I often use on the Waze navigation app, is the drive later option. To avoid wasting time in traffic jams on my commute home, I enter my destination around 3:00pm, for example, before leaving the office, then select go later. Waze offers various ETAs with departing and arriving times depending on your location and real-time traffic patterns. With this set-up, the app will send reminders and alert of the traffic pattern changes and the optimal time to depart as well as the potential time of arrival.

I remain in control of deciding whether I want to go, stay longer in my office to work on a project, or take a completely different route. Occasionally, an unexpected mishap will occur while I am on the road. When this occurs, Waze simply adjusts in real-time and offers recommendations that are based on current traffic conditions. Comparably, business decisions like an acquisition, or the launching of a new service could also be postponed and in such cases, data and analytics must remain your guiding principle in helping to provide accurate forecasts and evaluate whether to abandon your business decision or to move forward with it. It enables you to stay prepared for uncertainties and address them as they arise which results in proceeding with convincing evidence. A&T's acquisition of Time Warner in 2018 is a good example of my previous point. Despite the extended delays, A&T recognized the value of that acquisition and as a result, they stayed committed to finalizing the deal until a judge ruled in the company's favor. This came at a cost, but the deal if well-executed, "Would reshape the media landscape by uniting a telecom giant with the owner of CNN, Warner Bros., TNT, TBS and HBO," as Bloomberg[56] asserted back in 2017 following the judge's decision to delay the acquisition. This was due to the U.S. Justice Department's antitrust lawsuit.

Why Must Data and Analytics Become a New Mind-set?

The process of transforming your data and analytics strategy to a Waze-like advanced system will be a bumpy and complex road and a difficult learning curve. Since its initial release, the smart navigation app has evolved and remained at the cutting edge pace of advances in technology. It has embraced machine learning, deep learning and artificial intelligence—yet also remained engaged with its users as the driving force to its location-based data-driven ecosystem. The good news is you do not have to reinvent the wheel or start from scratch to become an analytics-driven organization. With that said, you must understand that your ecosystem will only be running as good as the data you feed into it. While there are a multitude of great tools to help you along the way, you are also going to require great employees that are able to strategically combine insights from data with experience and intuition in order to make the right decisions.

Analytics may not by itself resolve all your challenges; you will still have to take the necessary steps of first determining the location of your choice before being led on the road to success. While using Waze, you do not have to follow its real-time insights religiously, but you will at least be kept informed about what is happening, what is to come and what you can do about it. The analogy here simply infers that teams will succeed by understanding business complications, cross-cultural differences and sensitivities—building on their diversity, and knowledge of the industry. In addition to relying on their creativity, intuition, and experience — and using efficient insights from data to make smarter and faster decisions. Data-driven recommendations must ultimately be put into the context and scope of the responsibilities of an executive or manager's decision-making ability. With the acceleration of artificial intelligence (AI) and automation, these types of predictions will constantly be available to you as a manager in real-time and on the go. Your career and organization's future depend on how you apply critical thinking and make the right judgment calls. As a manager, you must be able to interpret and use these insights to foresee what is coming in your industry and make informed decisions about staying ahead of the competition and potential disruptors.

Contrary to Waze, where its drivers receive valuable insights to guide the navigation, not all advanced analytics systems are created equal. There are potential biases and risks that can possibly derail the system. In short, it is always wise to proceed with caution.

Leading the Way Towards Advanced Analytics

Talent matters. To take on the challenge and make the journey from descriptive, diagnostic, predictive and prescriptive analytics, you cannot solely rely on implementing an intelligent data and analytics ecosystem. While that is certainly important, it is not an adequate enough measure to ensure the successful transition of your company into the future. One must always keep in mind that technology solutions or intelligent systems will reflect, or design based on the diversity, experience, assumptions and the limitations of the team that conceives, designs, builds, trains, tests, and deploys them. With that said, in the digital age where a hashtag or glitch could significantly impact your career or damage your brand, it is important to pay more attention to cognitive bias in designing products or services—conceiving, writing and implementing algorithms—and particularly in collecting and selecting data to train artificial intelligence. Intelligent systems are as good as the quality of the data used to train them. I elaborate on this in subsequent chapters.

Get in the Game

The various types of advanced analytics might well be the secret engine or weapon behind companies like Amazon and Google who are always sprinting ahead of their competitors. It is quite astonishing if you are to simply pause and envision just how these companies often make data-driven decisions by using the most advanced techniques, the efficiency of machine learning, and the algorithms to constantly adjust and optimize their businesses operations and processes. It is like having the most advanced version of Waze aligned with their vision, culture and talent strategy directing them on what should be happening miles away. Consequently, they know just how to adapt, disrupt and reengineer their own business models which in turn enables them to make acquisitions as they see fit and ultimately develop the right products to sprint them miles ahead of their competitors. They might eventually get many things wrong, as they often do—but what is vital to their success is having a well-oiled analytics ecosystem to forecast and work towards what is coming next. They are always testing and building towards the future while their competitors are comfortable existing in the present or confined to the past.

Evidently, the power of descriptive, diagnostic, predictive and prescriptive analytics is not completely new. The "secret" is available at a very low cost to every company with the right strategy and talent that is willing and reinforced with artificial intelligence technology that was way too expensive to access just a few years ago. The organization with the team that fits into the changing landscape of digitalization will be well positioned to prevail in the future of work that is coming to us faster than we expected. It is important to underline that over reliance on complete automation could also lead to adverse results. I discuss this further in chapters 9 and 11. To get this equation just right, a well-balanced hybrid of human to machines is required along with an avant-garde strategy to leverage data and analytics in business operations.

Building Superminds Systems

This is a tedious learning process that requires strategic planning, active participation and collaborating with various business units, but the result will not happen instantly. Waze successfully integrates and models data generated from human interactions with road traffic and real-time events combined with cognitive computing in its ecosystem. The platform uses data and analytics to help over 100 million global users[57] navigate through complex traffic situations. It provides well-informed recommendations to consider while making real-time decisions throughout the journey to your destination. As you interact with your analytics ecosystem, the technology will continue to learn, model new trends, detect outliers, and patterns to appropriately adjust and evolve. Ultimately, it will only get better with time. How far along is your company? Are you ready to begin the process, and transform into the data and analytics driven workforce? The time is now.

Be very clear that this is a journey. Understand, validate and model the past into the future in order to effectively move forward. Be curious about where you were previously, how you got there and where you are headed to. Determine how to move forward and it becomes reassuring (with an efficient analytics system in place), to know that recommendations are always available and constantly adapting and evolving in real-time.

The Gut Zone–Lessons from the Top: CEOs At the Cross-road of Smart Leadership

Netflix: Visionary Ahead of the Game

On June 29, 2018, the share price for Netflix closed at about $391. The Wall Street analysts were celebrating its CEO, Reed

Hastings, as a great visionary. Consider however that in 2011, the CEO of Netflix foresaw the shortcomings of the DVD-by-mail business model, and decided to alter what had once been considered a very successful business by the market. That same year, the Dish Network bought Blockbuster,[58] the defunct company which was once the primary source of the movie rental business, in a bankruptcy auction. There was no instance clearer than the case of Blockbuster where failing to adjust to market changes and disruptions led it to the graveyard—a powerful example of what not to follow. Two years later, a *Reuters* article summarized the epic failure of the acquisition, "Dish Network closes all Blockbuster stores, lay off 2,800" employees. The article revealed "Dish has tried to tap the Blockbuster brand by unveiling a new Internet streaming service and a program to rent DVDs by mail, in a bid to challenge Netflix."[59]

Reed Hastings, as Time Inc. puts it, "Committed to streaming." The company's stock plunged 76 percent and even earned the headline as the worst performer in the market for a week. Wall Street vilified his plan citing it to be poor and unrealistic. Confident about his decision, he did not allow himself to be distracted from his vision and it paid off—big time. Netflix today, remains one of the most productive and successful firms in the business arena. Reed Hastings provided a solid path to an emerging business model—namely the subscription. This model has worked as a charm for Netflix as well as other enterprises that follow. In 2014, *Time* magazine reported that "87 percent of Netflix's revenue is derived from streaming movies and TV shows."[60] As of 2018, Netflix reached the 261st spot in the Fortune 500 with over $11 billion in revenue in 2017. This is a prime example of how "gutsy" leadership results in success!

Domino's: Leadership and the Impact of Data Informed Disruption

Domino's has more than 260,000 employees and reportedly operate in over 14,000 locations worldwide, as of 2017.[61] How far has the company come? Its share price closed at $282.17[62] on June 29, 2018—an incredible leap from $8.76[63] per share in 2010. This can simply be described as remarkable success. In short, the turnaround story is gutsy and began in 2010 when Domino's freshly appointed CEO, J. Patrick Doyle, realized that the only way out for the company was a complete revamp of its business model and branding strategy. This included a significant investment in its technology in order to transform the company's operations from a lane to an ecommerce powerhouse. Primarily, J. Patrick Doyle made the right gut call to digitally transform Domino's from its kitchen menus to the customer's doorstep. As a result, Domino's is considered as one of the "Top 10 companies in terms of online transactions, amongst companies such as Amazon and Apple."[64]

Merck: EQ, Empathy and Values

On occasion, a CEO's moral value, judgment and good leadership could be linked to its success. This holds true in the case of Ken Frazier, CEO of the multinational firm Merck & Co., Inc. Merck employs approximately 69,000 workers[65] and exceeded $175 billion in market value as of July 31, 2018—from $131.75 billion on October 31, 2013.[66] As one of the only 3 Black CEOs of Fortune 500 companies, Ken Frazier resigned from the White House's advisory council on manufacturing after the U.S. President made comments that were contrary to his company's values and personal convictions in the aftermath of a violent and disturbing white supremacist rally in Charlottesville, VA. Not only was it personal and demonstrative of great leadership, but it also influenced many other CEOs to follow suit. Ken Frazier explains his position in these terms, "As a matter of personal conscience, I feel a responsibility to take a stand against intolerance and extremism." In the words of Curt Nickisch during an interview with Ken Frazier on HBR IdeaCast "It's good to stand for something."[67] Under his leadership (since 2011), Merck with over $40 billion in global sales in 2017,[68] "Has produced more new medicines than any of its peer competitors."[69] According to Fortune 500, the pharmaceutical giant's "Superstar cancer immunotherapy" new drug Keytruda accounted for 15 percent of the company's sales.[70]

Microsoft's AI Experiment and Lessons Learned: The Art of Adjustment

Artificial Intelligence is not only still unfolding, but we are also still in an early process in which each step influences the next. If not implemented with care and caution, the system could tumble into a destructive mode and rapidly spin out of control. In 2016, Microsoft faced a similar dilemma after creating an AI chatbot, called Tay, that turned into a nightmare for the company. At issue, the artificial intelligence in less than 24 hours of interacting with users on Twitter started repeating racist and disparaging comments and quickly sent the public's opinion into a mode of frenzy. Microsoft swiftly reacted by deactivating it. CEO Satya Nadella, had little option but to apologize and take ownership of the mishap during the company's Build 2016 conference for developers. He promised to learn from the debacle and eventually fixed it. As a 2016 *MIT Technology Review* article reported, Satya Nadella acknowledged the fiasco, and indicated during the conference "We want to build technology in such a way that it gets the best of humanity, not the worst," and added "We quickly realized it was not up to the mark and so we're back to the drawing board."[71] This example is a somber reminder of what can go wrong when building AI systems and how to react and adjust effectively to make the difference. The appropriate course of action can prevent a simple wind from turning into the destructive tsunami that could wash away your organization. Microsoft set the perfect example on how to adjust. Despite its shortcomings, the company continues to learn from its mistakes and takes swift action when necessary. Microsoft remains one of the leading voices among technology companies that are promoting the necessity to carefully build AI systems that "Get the best of humanity." Microsoft continues to push the boundaries in new, inclusive and emphatic ways under the leadership of Satya Nadella. The CEO wrote the book on how to "Hit refresh" and did so at an interesting time for its enterprise. He is slowly setting the tech giant on a path to remain a leader of the future.

Wait! There Is More!

Though data is indisputable to an organization's success, gut decisions and leadership are required to make the hard decisions matter. From taking risks or making the decision to take the next exit on the journey ahead—your gut decision matters. Data is paramount, but it is important to make complex, risky and even costly decisions on occasion. Examples would be knowing exactly when to enter a new market or when to reengineer your business model. You can probably refer to a multitude of great examples to demonstrate gut decisions beyond the few selected cases that I have highlighted.

Other instances could be Mark Zuckerberg, (then only 22), who rejected a $1 billion offer from Yahoo to purchase Facebook in 2006. As of 2017, Facebook's revenue hit $40 billion. Ironically, in that same year, Yahoo was sold to Verizon for less than $5 billion while "Facebook exceeded $500 billion in market value."[72] Yet another case would be CVS Health's decision in 2014 to stop selling cigarettes and tobacco products. CVS wanted to prioritize health care spending and considered this decision as a good way of rebranding its image and repositioning the company as a primary health care brand. The tobacco ban impacted the company's bottom line and resulted in an estimated loss of a $2 billion drop in sales.[73] The following year, prescription sales continued to rise and CVS has since risen 2 spots to number 10 in the 2015 Fortune 500 companies with an annual revenue of $130.6 billion.[74] In the 2018 Fortune 500, CVS Health became the 7th largest U.S. corporation, based on its 2017 global revenue of $184,765 billion.[75]

Data and Analytics: The Gut Zone

Depending on your area of expertise, the decisions you make could sometimes be life or death situations. Consider a surgeon's timely decision of performing an operation that could be vital for a patient's survival. The cases described above were not life saving, however, the risk and timing of the decisions demonstrate strong leadership and gutsy calls at opportune moments. My point here is quite simple. Sometimes a leader might need to make business as well as personal decisions that could impact their career, the organization's market value or bottom line. Overwhelmingly, data demonstrates that when decisions are made in conjunction with the organization's values, strategic plans, visions, priorities, in addition to the people and culture supported by the reliable data—they get it right more often than not.

In the cases of Netflix and Domino's, both companies took different paths, but had one thing in common that continued to drive their success: they connected the dots, detected trends, identified outliers and patterns, and interpreted the data. They used the insights to understand what mattered to their customers and what could be disrupting to their business model. By streamlining the process and driving up their bottom line results and sales they have significantly improved the customer's experience.

There will be situations when a leader would need to make a choice that could have ripple effects (positive or negative). This could be either re-coding the business model, making an acquisition or expanding to new markets and shutting down a whole business division. These leaders had one thing in common: they trusted and relied on their gut. They did not walk on eggshells or put too much stock on the daily headlines. They were aware and mindful of what was at stake for their organization and the people they were leading. They played the game of risk and the strategy paid off for their employees, shareholders, and respective enterprises. They earned the success, yet just by looking at their current position, it may appear that they have unfair advantages as we tend to forget the difficult road they previously traveled.

PART THREE

DATA BECOMES AS PREVALENT AS OUR BREATH

6

Data Collection Essentials: Know What to Know

"Data is as important to a business operation's efficiency as water is to a human's thirst and body function. If you do not possess it, you must acquire it. If it becomes contaminated, it must be treated before further use. Failing to do so could cause a grave illness or even death. With that considered, it is safe to say that making data-driven decisions is a matter of survival for every business."

—Journel Joseph

We are in a period of constant and rapid change and it is complex and challenging to envision what the future will look like. We collect data and build powerful analytics systems under the assumption and probability that certain outcomes will occur, but more often than not, our projections go wrong. The systems, nonetheless, still matter. We are frequently limited by what we know, how we interpret past events, and our assumptions of unknown factors. While hard to predict, it is much harder to do nothing at all. Therein lies the need to build agile systems (as discussed in chapter 4) that are apt to adjusting in real-time to new conditions as events occur (the unpredictable, the rare event that will impact our forecast). The system is as good as our assumptions, and the data that feeds it. What we want to measure ultimately defines the data that we collect (qualitative or quantitative)—and what we measure serves to inform our business decisions, unearth opportunities or leads to systemic breakdown. If we are to consider these factors, understanding the process of data collection is paramount. The process does not happen in a vacuum. There is a lot of planning, and activities that is initially required. In this context, let us explore some of the basic standards of data gathering that go beyond the abstract. When we talk about feeding the system, perhaps a look at grocery shopping and a pantry inventory would aid in our comprehension of data gathering.

The Food Pantry: Understanding the Value of Data Collection

Consider a planned and organized grocery shopping experience for an upcoming family event. A very basic goal would be ensuring that time is spent very efficiently in the store to avoid purchasing unnecessary items. In order to achieve that goal, an itemized list of all the necessary ingredients would be required. This basic task will not only avoid a waste of time and effort, it would also mitigate the potential risks of over spending. The first step is creating a menu that would provide a great and lasting experience for your guests. For instance, if you are uncertain whether any of your guests may require gluten free or vegan meals, an inquiry must be made. In the same regard, data can be collected as you prepare to build your case for the usage of it. Data collection requires rigorous planning and discipline. It cannot and should never be conducted in a disorganized manner. In the same light, measuring or gauging the expectations of your esteemed guests, will require that you enquire what some of their favorite foods are as you are putting together recipe options. Consider and value your customers, patients or users in a similar manner. In the process of making your inquiries prior to conceiving menu options, you might also discover that some of your invited guests have food allergies such as shellfish. With that information, you could begin the process by checking your pantry to see what is available, required and which items may have potentially expired. Cooking with expired food items is extremely dangerous and can have adverse effects on your guests. Once the preliminary information collected from your guests, and the state of your pantry has been established, you can now conceive your cooking plan accordingly and generate a buying list of all the items based on your resources or budget.

The value of data collection is identical to the above illustration I have drawn in the nuance that often eludes organizations. Many companies often fail to incorporate these basic first steps of checking the pantry in gathering data for their projects. As a result, they purchase services that are not required and apply data that is not appropriate for their use cases. Consequently, they wind up building models with irrelevant data and their forecast eventually becomes a fiasco.

Next. Keep It Organized

It is essential to classify or group your list according to your menu. This will help you make a clear distinction on the items that need to be purchased as well as what is currently available in your pantry. The goal is to avoid buying unnecessary items if you are not disciplined. Additionally, if there is a tight budget in the equation, you may not be able cover all of the items needed. In some cases, you may need to consider finding items on sale and purchasing store brands, or making use of existing ones. Whatever the case may be, the plan is to avoid disappointing your guests with food that is subpar. With that in mind, it is important to focus on the quality of the items selected. Always keep in mind that the outcome can be costly without a well-defined and tightly organized purchasing plan. It requires discipline, rules that need to be followed, a planned recipe, and avoiding guesswork as you proceed. To some extent, this is a simple explanation of what data collection might look like in a nutshell. Pay attention to the principles.

Data Collection: 5 Basic principles:

1. *How you collect the data matters; always define and document your methods.*
2. *Protecting the data is a serious responsibility. Always ensure that data privacy by design is embedded into your practice—not as an afterthought.*
3. *Ask your subjects/customers to provide their consent when necessary—meaning inform and offer them choice and control, thus building trust from the start.*

4. *Improper processing and use of data will have serious consequences. Establish quality control (auditing) procedures to ensure reliability.*
5. *Be transparent and clear on how you plan to use and share the data.*

Data Collection: General View

If you are considering gathering data, it is essential to first think about the problem that you intend to solve, the specific questions you want to answer or the hypothesis that needs to be tested. To that point, you need to clearly define your use case to collect the data for your company's needs. It requires planning, time and resources to collect good and quality data. The process can get misconstrued without the proper protocol to help navigate your data collection methods. That said, you need to assess your business and investigate what kinds of problems, challenges or specific questions need to be addressed. Additionally, you will need to assess if the available data is suitable for aiding in your understanding of the problems that need to be determined and resolved. By using some basic insights as your starting point, you can begin to determine what is known. This form of understanding is necessary as we embark on the quest of the "know what to know" about data collection methods.

The most important aspect of data collection that should be carefully considered and valued is data protection and privacy. This will have serious implications for your organization or your project. As you proceed, it is important to design a data collection protocol that meets and safeguards your customers data privacy. In chapters 9 and 10, I will explore the global challenges to data privacy, with a focus on the European Union policy which is referred to as the General Data Protection Regulation (GDPR). It was established on May 25, 2018, and was conceived and designed to have an impact beyond the European Union countries. The GDPR has a strong enforcement mechanism with fines of up to 4 percent of a company's annual revenue.[76] Though it primarily targets EU citizens, the regulation sets the path to where the trend in data protection and privacy is moving. Similarly, in the case of the United States, California passed a landmark data privacy policy in June 2018.[77] It has become evident that many countries around the globe are drafting and reinforcing their current data privacy and security policies to protect their citizens and businesses. This is essential to understand as we move towards interconnected systems.

Data Privacy: A Business Imperative

To address potential uncertainties that will arise with the vagueness of data privacy policies across the globe, companies may need to re-code their business models in order to meet the increasing demand for privacy from their customers. Implementing the appropriate policies to catch up with these changes will take a significant amount of resources. The most effective approach would be to focus on data "Privacy by Design" (PbD) as a basic standard and have it incorporated into your business model. It is essential to note that the concept of Privacy by Design[78] (developed by Ann Cavoukian as the Canadian Commissioner of Information and Privacy in the mid-1990's), is not new and must become a business imperative for organizations in every industry. As Cavoukian puts it, "Privacy by Design begins with the understanding of both the value and benefits of adopting good privacy practices."[79] Data usage is unavoidable in every organization and is essential for the decisions and competitive advantage of your business. The collection of data requires you to follow practices that value the rights of your users/customers and design internal protocol to ensure compliance. Again, this is discussed at length in chapter 10, *A Roadmap to Data Protection and Privacy.*

As the CEO of Microsoft, Satya Nadella, put it during an interview on CNBC[80] with Jon Fortt, people value and want to be in control of their personal data and it comes down to the customer's trust in the business model of the company. Evidently, trust is primordial to survival in the digital age and a company's most important asset is its reputation.

A Note About Conventional Data Collection: What Does This Involve?

In this chapter, I predominantly explore "traditional" (established) data collection methods to help you understand the fundamentals, assess risk factors and uncover hidden opportunities as you move into digital transformation. What follows may not completely sound up-to-date when considering the cutting-edge of the big data processing technologies that are currently available. Understanding and focusing on the basics however, could prove to be essential for a solid foundation on data and analytics. Successive chapters of the book will take a deep dive into automated data collection, artificial intelligence, and the rise of interconnected systems, compliance issues, data quality and trust.

Although research indicates that digitalization has already transformed how we gather and analyze data, you will do yourself a disservice by skipping the conventional steps of data classification and collection methods. This cursory exploration might turn out to be the answer to ensuring that data protection and privacy leads to the adherence of established and tested best practices as well as theories and ethical codes of conduct that have long guided data collection.

So, How Do We Collect the Data?

I already initiated the process in the food shopping scenario. I will also present a practical experiment (related to the car rental industry), to help you explore how to uncover often overlooked opportunities in your data and grasp what is going on behind the scenes. Beforehand, let us explore the classification of data. This is an essential step to understand.

Data Classification

In the context of this book, data can be either classified as primary or secondary sources with some key distinctions.

Primary Data

Primary data (interviews, surveys, focus groups and digitized data collected from consumers, etc.), involves the process of collecting information directly from the subject or population for the purpose of a study, project or to gain primary insights to make informed decisions. This may involve, for example, conducting observations by watching students in a classroom, or patients in a hospital setting via filling out specific forms designed to gather relevant information on the subjects being observed. This could be as simple as a case of a business unit collecting primary data to capture valuable insights based on a specific use case through digital or traditional instruments.

Secondary Data

Data previously collected is stored and managed. Other researchers could analyze that same data (secondary) for various other projects or byproducts. This could be utilized for a different use case or to support or advance a similar purpose. In other words, secondary data refers to existing data that has already been collected and completed by another entity or even the same organization. There are varied types of secondary data, including administrative data such as public voter registration records for targeting campaigns or for canvassing, donor lists, medical records, and existing survey results. This refers particularly to longitudinal data sources such as panel studies and censuses. They can be accessed through government or national statistical agencies, universities, records and international institutions such as the World Bank Stats, UN Stats and Euro Stats. For example, the U.S. Census Bureau and data.gov provide important access to secondary data that can be used for a variety of projects or studies.

Types of Data Collection Methods

Data collection methods can be quantitative (obtainable in numerical values, measurable forms, generalizable and can be applied to make statistical inferences). They can also be qualitative (refers to narrative, non-numerical, exploratory answers). The type of methods used will be dictated by the specific research questions, the types of problems that need to be solved, use cases, timelines and resources.

In order to get started, it is important to understand that the questions you ask will guide your data collection process and the type and quality of the data you collect will define your findings. Those findings will be used to inform your decisions. Data gathering, regardless of its form or type is necessary in helping to uncover hidden values, testing a hypothesis, answering questions, understanding a specific issue and gaining valuable insights.

Quantitative and Qualitative Data Methods and Characteristics

"Data—qualitative and quantitative alike—are reductions of our experience...When we reduce our experience of those things to numbers, the result is quantitative data. And when we reduce people's thoughts, behaviors, emotions and environments to sounds, words, or images, the result is qualitative data."[81] —Bernard et al.

Quantitative Data

Quantitative data collection is the process of gathering data in a measurable and replicable form that can be used to analyze and interpret a statistical analysis and mathematical computations to make inferences and generalizations. Quantitative data provides insights to inform the designing of models, making predictions and the accuracy of forecasting. Common examples range from censuses to surveys, to observations and experiments as well as questionnaires that have closed-ended questions. They often require basic to complex sampling methods and an expertise in statistics and mathematical modeling techniques.

Qualitative Data

Qualitative data collection methods explore and seek to develop a deeper understanding of social phenomenon and behaviors as well as an explanation of the why of things. Qualitative methods include interviews, participant observations, focus groups, reviews, field notes, documents and visual and content analysis. They are less structured and may require a significant amount of time as the research team might consider using multiple data gathering methods to ensure the reliability of their results.

Mixed Methods

Mixed Methods can be defined as a third option that consists of the systematic integration of both the qualitative and quantitative methods. While it can be concurrent or sequential, this form of data gathering is often planned, designed and used to provide a broader picture of a phenomenon based on the research problems, questions and use cases.

Now, let us step back to the original foundation of the data collection methods previously discussed which would be the central premise of the next segment. The question to consider is whether to start from scratch or gather your own data with a simple sheet of paper. It is time to find out.

How Do We Collect Data?

There are a wide range of data gathering methods as described above. Each method of course, presents its strengths and weaknesses. Thus, it is critical to design a data collection protocol with a well-defined action plan and to determine resources that are available to execute your project and validate your process. You do not have to be an analyst to recognize the profound impact and value of data to gain insights that can help guide your business operations.

I want to underline that on a daily basis, you are collecting—from routine decisions of checking the price tags of items in the supermarket in order to save money, to planning your budget and checking your bank or credit card balance. And you have insights locked in your business operations. Though every decision you make in your business endeavor or practice may not always use the "most relevant" insights, it is based on the data you process which could be from prior experience or from the information you assume will generate a positive outcome. From now on, I want you to always be conscious and weigh your options. Develop abilities to assess and understand how you tend to make those decisions. What often drives them, and why? If executed correctly, this practice will soon become an integral part of your work and daily routine. This does not mean you should give up on what makes you unique (your intuition, creativity, gut, judgment, emotional intelligence, critical thinking and ethics). It is important to avoid becoming an automaton in the process.

What You Want to Measure Matters in a Rapidly Changing and Competitive Business Landscape

Data collection must be compiled using specific instruments, which entails the tools to capture the data. As a key component for efficient data gathering, it is essential to consider that the use cases, and questions you ask will most likely define the steps that need to be taken. Casting your nest too wide could be challenging without a clear target and a well-defined strategy.

To move forward, assume that you have determined what you want to measure, thus select your metrics and be ready to follow the subsequent steps. I want to reiterate that the questions you ask will define these metrics. As a *Harvard Business Review (HBR,* 2013) puts it, "You cannot pick your data, but you must pick your metrics."[82] If you make the wrong selection, the chances are you asked the wrong questions, then assessed the wrong metrics, and focused on the wrong use case. Getting this right will help you select the metrics that matter in order to have an in-depth understanding of your subjects.

As previously noted, the secret to data analysis beyond demonstrating relevant technical skills, depends on asking the right questions, defining a clear use case and being extremely curious with the unique ability to bring it all together. However, it is important to keep the process simple to avoid making it too cumbersome.

"A successful organization can only measure so many things well and what it measures ties to its definition of success."[83] —Harvard Business Review (HBR, 2013)

What is clear throughout the data collection process is that you need to follow systematic methods to gather the data and ensure its protection and privacy. With that said, just where do you start? To illustrate the process, let us push the boundaries in order to conduct an experiment that will demonstrate possible data collection scenarios in practice to inform business decisions.

An Experiment: Learning from the Data

Imagine this scenario: It is 8:45am and time to leave for a 10:00am meeting in Bethesda, MD. You have a flight scheduled to depart at 4:55pm from Ronald Reagan Airport (DCA) to Toronto, Canada. In addition to 2 other meetings in D.C. and

Alexandria, VA, respectively at 11:45am and 1:30pm. You may wonder what the most convenient and cost-efficient option would be to minimize travel time, traffic congestion, getting you to your meetings and finally to the airport beyond using a ride-sharing service yet maintaining control. The first step would be locating a suitable and affordable form of transportation that would cause less anxiety. The most interesting thing is that the service desired might already be available in an industry that is struggling with constant pricing competition to remain profitable in the ground transportation business. It turns out that customers have not only identified a suitable option, but they have also been utilizing it for years. To this point, this service is not being promoted as a business model to capitalize on the industry's competitive edge—so clearly, it is not maximizing its potential to succeed. This could be viewed as a hidden secret in a merciless business landscape in an industry possessing thousands of vehicles.

Insight from Inside: A Look at the Car Rental Industry

Consider the following case: a car rental executive, named Deidra Armstrong, notices that the industry has one of the lowest consumer satisfaction ratings with a Net Promoter Score (NPS) of 29 as compared to Tesla that had a NPS[84] of 97, which measures customer experience, feedback, and brand loyalty. Deidra immediately understands that customer satisfaction has to significantly improve and become a business priority for her company to survive.

Armstrong only came to that conclusion after the company's board asked her to conduct a data-driven assessment and propose some options to close locations in her district to reduce cost because of their low revenue. The company continually missed revenue expectations that had been forecasted by its analysts over the past few years. Instead, Deidra decided to connect the dots in the company's data to unearth untapped potential business opportunities. As a first step, she asked the analytics team to explore and provide relevant insights into the company's rental car fleet pricing model and rates, its transportation patterns and a complete breakdown of inventory management in the DMV area (District of Columbia, Maryland, Virginia). She instructed them to focus on the last 12 quarters (from 2014 to 2017) for a broad assessment. The findings showed a pattern related to car rental mobility from pick up to drop off locations across the three airports in the DMV area (DCA, BWI, and Dulles). She found that a growing number of customers were picking up vehicles from cities and dropping them off at different airports.

Insights: The Proof is in the Data

Deidra immediately discovers that the initial findings offer a strong opportunity to capitalize on. She envisions that promoting this service as an independent business unit would transform her company, and eventually the industry. First, she must use data to demonstrate the demand and build the case for a new business venture.

A Silver Lining in the Cloud

Considering that there is very little change in the car rental industry as it relates to the adjustment of competing business models, the data that is constantly being collected and stored has not been put to good use. Armstrong's bet seemed to pay off when she made the gutsy call to the board to table the plan. She shared that she discovered after analyzing the company's data that there could be great business opportunities that would expand the company's market and eventually increase its revenue. She admitted that they had not yet capitalized on the massive amount of data that had been collected and available for the company. She wanted to be sure that all of their options had been explored before taking the seemingly easy road. She asked for additional time and proposed that they conduct a more detailed study aimed at assessing the sentiment and the car rental usage behavior of their customers.

It is important to have a starting point. You can begin with your company's data, a report, social media findings, or even industry insights or secondary data. In this experiment, Deidra began her exploration with administrative data generated by the company's inventory management system. As it turns out, data collected over the years had been overlooked—and Deidra had to find potential solutions in the traditional business model as digital and disruptive entrants were transforming the industry. As a result, the business practice in the rental car industry had remained stagnant despite all the untapped opportunities revealed in the data. Bear in mind that your quest may occasionally lead to a dead end and that Deidra could have lost her job. This is the part of the process known as risk taking however, the data-driven insights will afford her the confidence to move forward with her decision.

Data Collection: Making the Case

At this stage, Deidra has a solid insight of pick off and drop off patterns for the rental vehicles. As a next step, the analytics team wants to investigate the data for travel patterns at the airports. A potential first step could be to identify the *secondary data* on the number of daily airport travelers across the DMV area. Government sources are reputable for such types of study. We could then begin with the following sources:

The Bureau of Transportation Statistics[85] (*Transtats Aviation Databases; Airline Traffic Data*) and Federation Aviation Administration (FAA), in addition to local and regional Airport Authorities. These agencies publish monthly and annual reports as well as fast facts on travel trends and patterns. All of this information is available in the public domain. The plan would be to identify relevant data points and insights to show the need to move forward. At this stage, Deidra and the analytics team have two strong relevant data sources that could support a potential business opportunity:

1. The company's data reveals a trend in drop offs at the airports. We can refer to this as baseline data which can be primary or secondary depending how it was collected.
2. The overall industry reports on passengers (secondary data).

Next Step: Triangulation

In order to complete what is described in the research field as triangulation[86] (techniques combining multiple methods of data gathering sources to enrich, corroborate, and validate findings)—Deidra and her team would need to collect additional data to understand the behavior of their customers. What must happen next? This will depend on the questions that she needs to investigate. In this case, Armstrong wants to understand her consumer and with sentiment analysis, she will be able measure the behavior patterns of her customers. To keep it simple, we will say the study protocol reveals that the research team needs to focus on 2 approaches:

1. Conduct interviews, surveys, personalization quizzes, or focus groups to ask customers directly. Once the population is identified, the plan will be to connect with them and select a sample size of those who have picked up vehicles from cities and dropped them off at airports. This process will entail developing an instrument that compiles primary data directly from those using the company's car rental service.
2. Monitor and collect social media posts and online reviews. You use web scraping tools to harvest the data that represents the opinions, and comments from customers about their experience or lack thereof. This process must follow a rigorous data privacy protocol (I elaborate on this in chapter 9). The results could lead to a significant industry innovation and potential disruption beyond the traditional business model. The car rental company could consequently gain greater agility in an industry that faces robust competition from disruptive entrants. This option although essential, has some limitations (the capturing context in which opinions were expressed as well as the current mood and mindset of the customer could reflect their curated views.) Additionally, some customers may not feel comfortable sharing relevant information about their experience on social media therefore, asking them directly through a series of interviews, surveys, or focus groups would help increase the accuracy of the study. Accordingly, the research team would also perform an in-depth analysis to assess and validate the data collected through social media depending

on available resources. The results could lead to a significant industry innovation and potential disruption beyond the traditional business model. In addition to extracting value to reimagine the car rental experience with innovative end-to-end products and services designed to reduce costs, increase quality, efficiency and flexibility—and to eventually provide some level of stability in a turbulent business environment. The car rental company could consequently gain greater agility in an industry that faces robust competition from disruptive entrants.

A Dying Industry: Betting on Data to Transform Its Service

The car rental industry needs a linchpin to hit refresh and take advantage of its existing assets. Their biggest competitive advantage is having offices in almost every convenient and visible major airport and city. Both of these attributes are powerful to the brand and by capitalizing and promoting this service, they are providing an exclusive option to their customers. Further, they would not need to invest in building that infrastructure. They would only need to create a digital experience and tap into their casting inventory which would help with their marketing costs. They could also build a cool ecosystem on demand service and even promote electric and semi-autonomous vehicles as an exclusive experience for this venture. That would be a winning strategy.

An interesting point, as previously indicated, is that they already have the option that allows a customer to pick a vehicle up from a city and drop it off at the airport. They might consider enhancing the service as a distinct business venture to accommodate customers even further. Making and promoting it as a formal business venture could boost their market values and revitalize the industry by showing that they can still be profitable. This scenario demonstrates how data can lead to the insights that will help re-code the car rental business model and take advantage of the interests and needs of the consumer in the modern day's car sharing economy.

Although this experiment is limited and its potential implementation would be more complex in practice—keep in mind that this is strictly conceived as a scenario to help you explore hidden opportunities in your company's data. What is evident, is that the car rental industry has not fully taken advantage of its best asset—its data. By promoting what I can refer to as an end-to-end "Sustainable and Flexible Transportation," Deidra will position her company to compete and remain relevant in the future of mobility as we cruse into interconnected systems, smart cities that will be powered by a network of digital infrastructure (data and analytics, 5G technology, intelligent design, IoTs, sensors and autonomous vehicles).

Perspective

Once the data is captured and stored following the established protocol, there are a few options remaining that will depend upon the amount and types of data collected. The primary focus is to prepare, code and ready that data in a format for analysis. You can choose some simple analytics options that would allow you to categorize and handle your data and gain the insights to act upon or you can focus on complex modeling techniques and use sophisticated analytics tools. The action will be dictated by your resources and the skilled-analysts that are available. You would need to understand which factors are most likely to bring success to your business operations and how to unearth valuable insights to inform your business decisions in a highly competitive and disruptive industry. It is important nonetheless, to ensure that the process follows three simple rules which are essential to guaranteeing and maintaining the integrity of your project and outcomes. Always remember that the data is **accurate**, **reliable** and **relevant** to your use case. These are three essential check points to pass through when collecting or harvesting data regardless of whether it is quantitative or qualitative.

Your Business Operations Are as Good as Your Data and Your Team

The technical landscape may have changed with digitalization, but the process remains the same. The distinction of data types (qualitative and quantitative) is important to keep in mind as we move forward to subsequent chapters. Regardless of the route you choose to gather data for your project, you must consider the type of methods to use and this is critical at every stage of the data collection lifecycle. The key for this distinction is to simply understand how the data was gathered and how viable or reliable it is. You have to identify how you access the data and document and explain the methodology used for its collection when disseminating your findings. Regardless of whether you are using qualitative or quantitative data, it is still essential to clarify if there are any privacy issues. You most certainly do not want to incorporate any data that could put your organization at risk.

Advances in technology makes the path increasingly automated and inevitable in enriching research studies and outcomes. This will also require navigating the ever-increasing challenges that are related to data privacy and quality control. This is essential and powerful because establishing an efficient study design in addition to sound data collection practices and analysis could define the validity and reliability of a study. For example, a properly conceived study could save lives and improve the well-being of a community. Society, businesses, and researchers will all be negatively impacted in the long run if we ignore the concerns about data protection, trust and privacy. In the next chapter, I will breakdown 2 of the most widely used data collection methods; namely, **survey** and **focus group**. I will also share some personal stories on how you might apply them through traditional or digital data gathering techniques. As a cautionary note, it is important to keep in mind that the goal of building machine learning models is to include features or attributes with predictive information not for the sake of using massive amount of data—what matters most is the quality of the data and not its size.

7

Data Collection Strategies: How Far We Have Come?

"The most important aspect of data collection that should be carefully considered and valued is data protection and privacy. This will have serious implications for your organization or your project. As you proceed, it is important to design a data collection protocol that meets and safeguards your customers data privacy."

—Journel Joseph

Insights generated from data can lead to moments of truth. They could be the discovery of hidden values or signals that uncover the areas of fault within your business operation or they can even detect the decrease of revenue. Insights have also been known to develop a treatment or form of therapy to cure a disease. Overall, it is fair to say that data can transform your organization and has already transformed our lives. It dates back from the first reported U.S. Census conducted in 1790,[87] nearly ("A year after the inauguration of President George Washington").[88] Data collection has always been used to help inform decisions over centuries, even before the first census taken in the United States. Census as a form of data collection serves as a guide to world's history, and play vital role in development, as the U.S. Census Bureau describes it, "the census tells us who we are and where we are going as a nation. The census helps our communities determine where to build everything from schools to supermarkets, and from homes to hospitals. It helps the government decide how to distribute funds and assistance to states and localities. It is also used to draw the lines of legislative districts and reapportion the seats each State holds in Congress."[89]

Briefs: Survey and Focus Group in the Golden Age of Digitalization

Quantitative Data Collection Methods–Brief: The Survey

This data collection method is characterized by structured questionnaires and uses rating scales to capture the voice of your customer. Designing surveys can be a complex undertaking and requires diverse skilled researchers for a broader perspective, depending on the magnitude of the study. The survey design process involves procedures of developing a scale as theorized by Rensis Likert (1932)[90] containing multiple items, which typically ranges between a four and seven-point scale (response choices). Paul E. Spector, in his book, *Summated Rating Scale Construction: An Introduction*, covers and defines the relevant steps of scale development from determining how to select the number of items to the response categories. As he puts it "These scales are widely used across the social sciences to measure not only attitudes, but opinions, personalities, and descriptions of people's lives and environments as well." He also indicates, "Scales presently exist that measure emotional states (e.g., anger, anxiety, and depression), personal needs (e.g., achievement, autonomy, and power), personality (e.g., locus of control and introversion), and description of jobs (e.g., role ambiguity and workload)."[91] Designing surveys requires skill in statistical analysis methods and the strong expertise to design clear, unbiased and consistent questions that are easy to read and understand. The proof of a good survey lies in the construction of the questions and the rating scale, and requires researchers that are skilled in survey design.

Planning Stage

The initial stage requires one to determine what they want to measure. This is the first step in ensuring that there is a focus on what is relevant and matters in order to secure successful feedback from your customers. The planning stage of a survey is a daunting task. It entails following certain key imperatives to engage in the best practices. As a manager, you must develop an expertise to assess the scale of the challenges as they arise and define strategies to turn them into new sources of a competitive advantage. Asking the right questions will lead to valuable insights and increase customer engagement which in turn will create unlimited business potentials for your organization. In many cases, you might just be better off using an instrument or questions that have already been validated.

Over a decade ago (2006), I was involved in the lengthy process of designing a global survey that was going to be tested and implemented across various countries in Europe, the U.S. and the Middle East. Just a few months prior to that experience, I was offered a position at a company where I Interned as part of an Assistantship following a 2-year training in Program Evaluation and Applied Research (a program funded by the NSF, which is the National Science Foundation.) During the course of my training, I developed a profound interest in instrument development due to my training and conferences attended across the United States. My supervisor recommended that I join the team due to my level of interest, and my previous work. My multicultural and multilingual background led her to believe that I would be a good fit. The team was equally as diverse and included practitioners, scholars, experts and graduate students. This went well beyond what I had learned in my training, conferences and early practices. I was amazed at the process it took to test each question as well as the procedure required to request permission to use already validated ones. It was real and very intense. It took endless hours and months of conference calls, meetings and work sessions just to design and finally validate the process. To be clear, not all surveys require that level of rigor and detail. The point however is that a good survey must be carefully planned and designed according to a well-defined study protocol. Over the years, I have analyzed, read, tested and validated surveys ranging from a basic paper and pencil method all the way to an advanced digital format. Additionally, I have compiled tests for large projects and helped conceive and design the databases to store them. Surveys play a significant role in data collection and every discipline and industry from government to business have used them. We are often asked to complete them following our interaction with a site, after receiving services, an experience with a call center, or even interaction with a customer service representative. Our experience is also sought after via email requests, mobile devices, social media platforms or even the web, after a stay at a hotel or a meal at a restaurant. Our insights matter and are used to help improve how we receive services. That said, it all depends on the types of questions being asked as well as the design of the instrument—which makes it absolutely critical to getting the process right. Located below in very simple terms is a look at 7 of the key principles that I have learned, researched and studied that will serve you. The purpose is to clarify the crucial role that surveys play in informing the decision making process and why it is essential to follow well-defined guidelines.

"In addition to sampling errors, one should bear in mind that question wording and practical difficulties in conducting surveys can introduce error or bias into the findings of opinion polls."[92] —Pew Research Center

Essentials of Survey Design and 7 Core Principles

To begin with, identify and describe each topic in a clear, non-misleading way and follow it up with relevant questions. The next step is to define the purpose of the survey and what the results will be used for. Follow these 7 steps as the guiding principles. Be sure to focus on what matters; keep your survey simple and short because the response rate could decrease depending on the length of the survey. Each extra unnecessary question could lead to the decline of the response rates. Next, when using a digital platform—set up your survey in a format that would permit a respondent to skip questions and only answer those that are relevant to them.

In addition, consider including follow up questions in some cases in order to collect actionable insights from users or customers. This can be achieved by asking or including simple subsequent questions and a description box or space for filling out responses. Do not overlook this additional step as it can lead to important opportunities to gain valuable information about loyal or dissatisfied customers and their sentiments and perceptions about your business. This information could lead to valuable insights that will aid in improving the customer's journey and overall experience.

Survey Design: 7 Core Principles

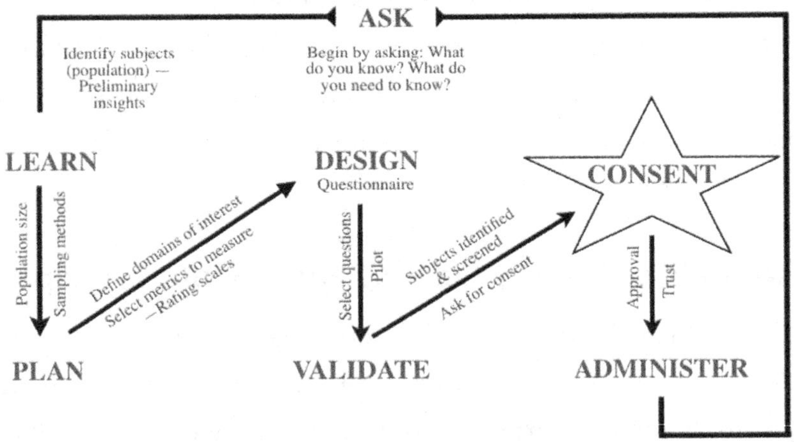

Ask: The questions you ask will in turn define the findings—you must always bear this in mind. Writing clear, concise and neutral questions are crucial. Although this is an essential rule, it is insufficient. An important barometer to use in gauging the proficiency of your survey is performing a consciously unbiased assessment of the questions. This consists of a diagnostic approach to unearth the hidden or confounding perceptions of the researchers that could influence how the questions are asked. First, begin with the following questions: What do you know? What do you need to know? The unknown will follow.

Learn: At the core of survey design is your ability to learn. Once you identify the population—you must learn as much about your subjects as you can before selecting the sample size to conduct the survey. Your survey cannot happen in a vacuum and the questionnaire must be informed by the prior insights that your research has discovered. This could be in the form of literature reviews, interviews, focus groups, research study findings, reports or other survey results. This process could begin for example, with focus groups or interviews and using those findings to inform the design of your survey.

Plan: Understanding the methodology that you plan to adopt matters. Ensure that the methodology is transparent and easy enough to comprehend and replicate during the planning phase. Another important factor is to divide or classify your questions into domains or categories with key themes. Accomplishing this will assist in defining the order and organization of the questions. This will also aid in simplifying the coding and analysis process. Finally, be sure to design and utilize a survey protocol that will serve as a guide and reference point. Do not include personal identifiable information (name, address, IP address, or other personal identifiers). It is highly recommended to use ID codes. That said, anonymization of personal data will help in minimizing risk and ensuring personal privacy.

Design: Proceed by formulating the questions and defining the measurement scale to use. Be sure to take cultural awareness and sensitivity into consideration. Additionally, it is crucial to pay close attention to the wording of the questions and the key concepts. Avoid context effects; it takes only one poorly conceived question to derail your project, skew the survey results, harm your subjects, or even impact your career. Avoid acquiescence bias. Designing surveys involves many challenges, particularly in the digital age where one hashtag can spark a revolution. This is why there is the need to have a diverse and well-qualified team that are using the best practices during the process in order to avoid pitfalls.

Validate: Secure input from a diverse group as a pilot to pre-test your survey to ensure reliability and relevance in addition to addressing any potential issues.

Consent: Obtain consent from subjects beforehand and inform them on how and what their data will be used for.

Administer: There are many options to distribute and administer surveys. **Paper:** This can be defined as the basic pen and pencil technique. **In-person:** They take on the form of onsite interviews and field surveys and often involve testing—such as drawing blood from respondents for medical panel studies. **Digital:** This technique could be used in the format of In-App surveys, SMS, emails and web platforms such as Survey Monkey, social media and mobile devices.

Using survey methods to gather data is widely used across every industry and field. With the rise of digitalization, surveys can now be conducted with a large number of respondents via web, mobile and electronic mail.

Quite often, a survey method involves collecting data from a large number of subjects which could be impracticable or costly to accomplish, hence the development of sampling. I will cover this very important stage of data gathering below.

Sampling

Samples can be chosen according to various criteria. What is important to remember is that efficient data collection is built on the quality and relevance of the samples selected. The research team must define a protocol to guide their sample selection methods. This is necessary to avoid the process of becoming biased by the personal judgment of researchers. In the preceding section, I will cover how to estimate an adequate sample size for your project or study. Before then, let us take a cursory look at what a sample size consists of and why it matters.

There are varied constraints such as cost and time that could make it impractical or impossible in many cases to survey, for example, the entire millennial population in the United States. This creates the necessity to use an alternative and reliable method to select a sample—a manageable size of the population. This is known as a sampling method. When well executed, this method can be used to make predictions, inferences and forecasts of future outcomes. Simply put, sampling consists of selecting a representative group from the population that you want to investigate. A small enough group that would make a study feel doable, yet big enough for the solutions or results to make a difference and finally, significant enough to infer broader outcomes. Since there are many great textbooks and MOOC courses that focus on the techniques and mathematics of sampling, I will not internalize on the substance detail. What I have provided below is a quick reference of a few methods. Consider researching them as you move forward in this journey.

Sampling schemes vary from non-probability sampling to probability sampling. Non-probability sampling consists of voluntary sampling, quota sampling, snowball sampling and convenience sampling. This technique is often used when the population being surveyed in not well defined, or for an exploratory study or a test and findings could be biased—statistical inferences should not be made. Probability sampling consists of random sampling, stratified sampling, cluster sampling, multistage sampling and systematic random sampling. Using this technique aids to minimize bias and all members of the identified population have an equal chance to be selected, and statistical inferences can be made. What is important to know is a good sampling must constitute a representation or a match of the population's characteristics. This suggests that the findings that are generated from the selected sample must reflect the insights that would have been produced from surveying the entire population.

Population size: consists of the total number of the group or subjects you want to study. Let's consider a sample of millennials to briefly illustrate its application. According to the U.S. Census Bureau population data, millennials (born between 1981 to 1996) were approximately 71 million in 2016.[93] If you were to study the voting or purchasing behaviors of this demographic group, your population size would be approximately 71 million. From that group, you could select your study participants by using sampling methods. This will require thorough planning because millennials are very diverse at many levels and are influenced by varied confounding factors that could be hard to measure. Conducting a survey alone may not provide an adequate understanding of their behavior, interests and motivation which would result in unreliable inferences about them.

Recommended sample size selection: In percentage points (at 95 and 99 in 100 confidence level).[94]

In addition, it is important to assess how margins of error and confidence level affect the accuracy of your results. Below is a cursory illustration.

	Confidence Level 95%		Confidence Level 99%	
	Margin of Error		Margin of Error	
Population size --)	5%	1%	5%	1%
10,000	370	4,900	623	6,247
50,000	382	8,057	657	12,486
90,000	383	8,679	661	14,045
150,000	384	9,027	663	14,980
500,000	384	9,423	665	16,106
1,000,000	384	9,512	666	16,369
5,000,000	385	9,586	666	16,586
25,000,000	385	9,601	666	16,630
75,000,000	385	9,603	666	16,638

Source: Survey Monkey: Sample Size Calculator

Margins of error: This refers to a percentage that indicates "How much you can expect your survey results to reflect the views of the overall population. The smaller the margin of error, the closer you are to having the exact answer at a given confidence level."[95] As previously indicated, depending on the type of study and the population you examine, a triangulation approach may be required to ensure that you make an accurate inference about the population.

Confidence Level: Is the expression of how confident you are about the sample accurately reflecting the total population that you want to draw conclusions from. The larger the sample size, the more comfortable you will feel about your results. This process however can be costly and as you include bigger sample sizes, it is important to make decisions according to your budget and the other resources available to your study.

Qualitative Data Collection: Beyond the Numbers

"The qualitative researcher has an obligation to be methodical in reporting sufficient details of data collection and processes of analysis to permit others to judge the quality of the resulting product." —Michael Quinn Patton

The methods used to collect data that could lead to a more thorough understanding of human behaviors, feelings, sentiments, attitudes and perception about products, services, brands and so much more. Qualitative data allows for an in-depth exploration and a deep dive into the hearts of the respondents' views. It also offers a useful tool for really understanding the pain points of your customers beyond the numbers. Qualitative methods require an expertise in designing instruments, defining thematic coding to capture the perception as well as the why behind a customer's behavior and feelings about your brand. Qualitative data refers to content that can be categorized as a non-numeric value. What immediately follows is a briefing on the relevance and essentials of a focus group which is one of the qualitative data collection methods. Improving the customer experience is vital for your enterprise's success and focus groups can offer an insight to their perception and feelings about your product or service.

Brief: Conducting Focus Groups

What Is a Focus Group? Why Even Conduct One?

A focus group is a moderated discussion involving a small group of participants. They are often constituted of between 4 to 8 individuals as a general principle. This has proven to be one of the most effective and manageable numbers to efficiently facilitate the flow of conversations. A well-planned, organized and moderated focus group can help capture relevant insights about the subjects or the views of the target audience as well as their perceptions, opinions, feelings, attitudes, beliefs, ideas and experiences. Focus groups can be used to inform the design of other data collection methods, to test public opinions, assess the perception of customers or their interest in a new product or service. In this chapter, I elaborate on this using real-life and practical examples. It is an important component in market research to learn about your target audience. It is almost indispensable in marketing strategy. As you are reading this brief however, you should bear in mind that focus groups have their limitations.

Focus Groups: An Overview

Focus groups allow you to receive direct and unfiltered data that could change the outcome of a product or service. Participants can be selected from subjects involved in a study or from new users that are identified after testing, experiencing or using a product or service. The selected participants must reflect your intended target market or demographic profile. Having less than 3 participants in a focus group is not recommended and should never be considered. By the same token, exceeding 10 participants in a focus group, could make the flow of discussion hard to control and the respondents may have inadequate time to freely express their opinions and ideas or share their experiences. It is preferable to conduct multiple focus groups to have deeper insights and to better inform your use case.

Let us use the example of handling dozens of focus group sessions with ease. You may be confident in your ability and facilitation skills, but how do the dynamics change when it comes to moderating sensitive topics? What happens when the room expands across geographic locations and what measures will you undertake to ensure data privacy in the digital age? These questions are critical and demonstrate how the process can become complicated and require innovative solutions. Most importantly, your approach must be grounded in the best practices. In this brief, I assess the risks and opportunities for conducting focus groups, examining the varied dimensions as well as the complexity of the subjects. Additionally, I will explain how to maintain the core value of your participants and how to develop the awareness to deal with potentially uncomfortable situations.

Opportunities and Limitations: What You Need to Know

Let us imagine that as a retail company, you were interested in testing the market for a new platform for a delivery service. You could benefit from conducting a series of focus groups with your targeted customers. In this case, I recommend that you use preliminary insights to design the focus guide (tool) such as a behavioral analysis. This is a fundamental principle for the conception of an efficient focus group guide.

You can begin by exploring the data of specific demographic groups that your initial findings reveal are more likely to use the service. You need to understand your customers first before proceeding any further. Alternatively, you can focus on the hard to reach customers (they could be interested, but are inactive because they do not have a need for what you are asking just yet), and even target customers who might seem reluctant to use the service to gain insight and understand your audience. These discussions can help you determine what customers or users perceive as trends and how they view your brand or products.

Limitations

The designing of a new product or service may fall well beyond the frame of its limits and more often than not, focus groups appropriately fulfill their intended purpose. I want to underline that it is quite complicated. As Steve Jobs demonstrated, focus groups may not always be the panacea and from that standpoint, his thought process was spot on. It is rather challenging to ask customers to share their views or feedback on products they can neither imagine nor have little insight on. Another notable example would be Henry Ford who famously stated that if he had asked customers what they wanted while designing his vehicles, they would have indicated wanting “A faster horse”. The message here is that results or feedback from focus groups are indeed limited consequently, your business will have to determine whether or not to use them. Although the Steve Jobs and Henry Fords of the world are geniuses that appear perhaps every century, their approach did not disqualify focus groups or market research. It is left to you to understand the territory of innovation and disruption and to understand that focus groups are useful when required to validate a product or service.

There are other embedded options that permit you to collect and analyze data in real-time from customers. Going back to Steve Jobs, let us reflect on when he introduced the iPhone 3G—the second version of the iPhone on stage. He demonstrated the use case for the updated version by referring to the data collected from users of the first iPhone. He indicated that the first iPhone had a 90 percent customer satisfaction rating and noted that 98 percent of the usage involved mobile web browsing while 94 percent were using email, 90 percent were text messaging and 80 percent were using 10 or more of the phone’s features.[96] Further, he went on to present new products, including the third-party applications that would change our lives forever.

Conducting Focus Groups: Identifying and Screening Participants

When conducting focus groups, the use case should be limited and focused unless your intent is to use insights generated from these focus groups to develop or inform other instruments such as surveys, interview or observation guides. That said, it is essential to define the purpose of your focus group. Keep in mind that the use case will help define the prospects or demographics you intend to target.

How Do You Select Participants?

The research team must define the characteristics of potential subjects or prospects. Let us assume that we make a rational choice for instance, to select participants from the segment of our customer base that shows interest and seems comfortable with using digital platforms. Our choice is dictated by the phenomenon that is being studied—which is our purpose in this case. Gaining insight will inform our design and enhance the user experience (UX). I elaborate more on this below.

Screening

The process of screening is important and time-tested as it involves differentiating your target population based on specific and pre-defined attributes. Screening tools are widely used in various settings and can range from the questionnaires that are given to respondents with embedded tests or a simple registration form to capture relevant information about prospective participants. In this experiment, let our target population be defined as "active customers ranging from the ages of 29 to 49 who are married and single professionals." You have to identify a cut off period which we will select as customers who have been active for at least six months. This will result in some background and investigative work to come up with an exhaustive list. You could use administrative data, such as your company's database of shoppers, assuming that you collect data on their purchasing behavior and frequency. This will require that you screen your customers and classify them based on selected and pre-defined criteria that are relevant to the project. If such data is not available, as is often the case, your next course of action should be to ask the customers directly. This can easily be achieved by providing them with a simple questionnaire to complete with all the right incentives. Be sure to tell your customers in the process, why you want the data and how it will be used. It is imperative to always seek their consent first.

Developing the right tool to collect data at every critical milestone in the journey will play an essential part of the process in ensuring that you have the appropriate group of subjects to select from.

Strategic Observation

Once you have secured your cross-generational demographics, it will give you the opportunity to design your guide with the intent of capturing any potential differences in risk tolerances, behaviors, interests and preferences as to how and when they interact with the platform. It is important to explore how the demand or interest in your service varies across the demographics. Assume in this case that you are investigating potential opportunities and unmet needs rather than testing or validating the quality of a service.

To keep our experiment exciting, let's suppose you started working on the platform by taking the approach of "if you build it, they will come," but suddenly seem to reach an impasse. You then decide to go back to the basics for the next step or proceed with a complete reconfiguration of the user experience. You are ready to go and start over based on the findings that will be generated from your focus groups, administrative data and surveys. With this course of action, you are committed to letting your insights dictate your next step. This next step should enable you to gain insights into your customers' interests which will be essential to conceiving and asking the right questions in order to collect the data that is relevant to your case.

During this process, let us say for example that you are also testing whether or not you are heading in the right direction. You would need to select relevant quality and process metrics to benchmark performance, track usage, test efficiency—measure failure rate and defect frequency, evaluate activities across demographics groups—and use the insights to improve the design of your digital platform. You cannot solely rely on a focus group in this instance, to inform your decision. For the next step, you could plan to test your customers with their consent by sharing your digital platform with embedded options to track and measure their usage patterns and collect the data to help inform the iteration of the service—and conduct follow up focus groups to gain additional insights. Focus groups can be used at various stages of the development and life cycle of a project, product or service—however, it is important to define relevant and appropriate use cases. The bottom line is it is an important time-tested practice to gauge your customers.

Focus Group: A Personal Journey Back in Time and a Look Forward

I have come a long way and have always been self-conscious about how using technology can improve data collection. Over a decade ago (2006), I was part of a group of students being trained in Program Evaluation and Applied Research (previously mentioned). I led a team dispatched to conduct focus groups with students at a Boston charter school. Upon arrival, the team assembled the participants, follow the protocol and began the discussion. Shortly after, the colleague responsible for recording one of the focus groups, failed to turn on the tape recorder. As the moderator, I was so in-tuned with asking the questions, which was my role, that I did not give it a second thought. Later that evening, much to my surprise, I discovered the blunder after receiving the (cassette) tapes and checking the recording to transcribe the discussion for our next meeting. We had left the room without bothering to check in order to get to our respective activities. Needless to say, what followed was short of pleasant. Our professor, Dr. Anna Madison, proceeded to lecture the entire team indifferent about who had actually committed the blunder. I can safely say that the lecture, to put it nicely, was a stern rebuke. Professor Madison, a renowned scholar—who at the time had over 30 years of experience as an instructor and practitioner, indicated that we had a very serious responsibility as researchers to appropriately handle the data collected from our subjects. She further emphasized that failing to record the session was unacceptably careless—it was not a pleasant moment for the team. The look of disappointment on her face was enough for me to completely understand the gravity of the situation. She went on to say that this would be an important lesson learned. Going forward, we should always be conscious of our responsibilities and make sure that a mistake like this never happened again in the lifetimes of our careers unless we planned to seek alternate lines of work.

Over the years, I have been at (almost) every stage of the data collection and analysis process—from traditional methods to using advanced data gathering and digital tools (APIs, scraping algorithms, emails, the web and more). This experience was particularly devastating for me as the team leader. I became extremely cautious about what could go wrong to the extent that it became somewhat of an obsession. I began using 2 tape recorders and placed them in positions where I could actually see the tapes rolling. I have traveled overseas and to many places in the United States and conducted hundreds of focus groups and interviews with a keen awareness of my sessions being taped. I valued every moment of listening to the subjects sharing sensitive information over the phone or on tape because they were entrusting me with the great responsibility of handling their data. I followed these same principles when designing and implementing advanced data collection tools for small or large projects with the same rigor for data protection and privacy.

About 2 years after the infamous failed recording experience, I was working at a global research company in Boston. Our center decided to use telephone interviewing to collect highly sensitive health data for projects funded by one of the world's premiere pharmaceutical companies and other projects sponsored by the National Institutes of Health (NIH). I remembered the debate about the practicality and reliability of collecting data over the phone and quickly settled down after conducting a few interviews. The technology soon served to remove geographic restrictions and allowed the participants to be at ease to share their personal feelings and experiences about topics varying from sexual health, diabetes, pain, mental behavioral studies and more.

In the real world, we often have no margin for error and the price to pay can be costly. As a result, I always ensured that the new recording technology worked, and never failed—not even once. I am always exploring the next breakthrough or algorithm that will help improve my technique. The technology made it possible to process data, code, clean up, model and finally analyze it. We are on the verge of breaking new ground in research studies with the advancement of technology as previously discussed in this book. My experience and interests from the analog tape recorder to digitalization and automation has continued to guide my thinking over the years. Although, we are still in the early days, I am convinced that groundbreaking mixed reality technology will change how we learn, interact and even conduct surveys, interviews and focus groups in the near future. And blockchain technology will soon revolutionize how we record, store, secure, share, process, tract and validate data.

The technique of telephone interviewing which initiated over a decade ago, has increased the number of participants and expanded our reach across geographic boundaries. It has also cut travel costs and saved the companies a great deal of money. Perhaps the new virtual experience will significantly increase the interest and participation of focus groups, surveys and interviews and eventually enable brands to gain valuable insights to informing or guiding their decisions. The new age of technology is coming—and it may be sooner than expected. Despite it all, I have to admit that nothing can replace the thrill of sitting at a table and moderating a focus group or interviewing a subject the old fashioned way.

Moderating a Focus Group: How to Make It a Success

The success or failure of a focus group depends largely on the effectiveness and leadership of the moderator. (Assuming you have a well-designed guide with relevant questions.) The most important role of an interviewer or facilitator is to gain trust and make the participants feel comfortable enough to share their opinions. A skilled moderator or facilitator is paramount in ensuring that the participants are comfortable, at ease, and fully engaged to share their views or opinions. The moderator must take the time to strategically prepare the participants before the conversation. Most importantly, they must ask and record their consent (verbal or written) as an essential step in the process of building a rapport and level of trust with them. Additionally, the facilitator must provide clear and concise details as to how the data will be used and how it might improve the well-being of the subjects or their society at large. In some cases, depending on the study, a moderator might decide to go back to participants to share the results and ask for additional feedback.

Groundwork: Participant Selection and Readiness

Depending on the types of study or purpose, you can ask selected participants to come prepared with some ideas on the topic beforehand—this could be useful in product development. Further, this could play a pivotal role in reinforcing your findings. It could help prevent the potential flaws of asking participants to provide their insights based on their memory of using the product or service in question. A customer's memory can become faded by the time of the study which is why tools that allow real-time insight into a customer's behavior have attracted such interest and investments. They provide the ability to measure what the participant is doing or thinking in the moment.

It is essential to ensure that you give each participant adequate time to share their view and avoid letting a select few monopolize the discussion. Keep in mind as you are dealing with these individuals that their personality and style will be reflected during the sessions. An introvert may not feel as compelled to answer each question or to be as talkative as an extrovert. Some moderators might encourage or even require each participant to share their thoughts on each question. This strategy can be very effective if conducted properly, however it is advisable to not make the participants feel as though they were being quizzed or formally interrogated. Keep a smooth flow of conversation and try to lean towards the person speaking. Always adopt an enthusiastic tone when asking questions or probing and use ice breakers when necessary to lighten the mood if you are comfortable and able to. An effective facilitator knows what to do when the discussion feels stalled or too tense. They should also have the ability to understand the audience through empathy and awareness. Discussions about sensitive topics can be challenging to moderate. As a starting point, you must take the time to do your homework and get to know your audience. Be present in the discussion to avoid those weird or awkward moments that might emerge. It is also important to acknowledge potential risks to participants and prepare them for it. A great moderator must be able to demonstrate and integrate Emotional Intelligence (EQ) while facilitating focus group discussions. It is crucial to remember that how you say something can have more impact than what you actually say. Evidently, some of these important characteristics may not be transferable when using a virtual room.

What EQ Has to Do with It?

It has *everything* to do with it. It can make or break the process. **Self-awareness** is essential for being in the moment and remaining calm and collected. Manage your emotions and that of your participants. You must handle stress and potential conflict by controlling your body language. In an in-person focus group or digital setting or even the tone of your voice can send different messages. Know when to probe for deeper, thought-provoking answers without pushing it—stay in your lane to facilitate the conversation rather than leading or taking it over. Practice comfortable signs (to let each participant speak and end a final thought), without brisk interruptions to move to the next question. Finding the right moment is essential. You can nod your head, smile or offer a "hmm," for example. Overall, being a great facilitator is an art, you have to know exactly what to do. **Social awareness** is required in order to pay close attention to a participant's behavior as well as learning to read their emotional cues. This will aid in creating a comfortable ambiance and making them feel completely at ease. It will also depend on the moderator's ability to forge a relationship and to demonstrate empathy, an understanding of cultural differences and the knowledge of how to code switch. **Self-management**, simply put, indicates the need to demonstrate restraint and to avoid being too involved beyond facilitating the discussion.

EQ is only a basic part of moderating a good focus group. Also required would be a well-planned and designed guide that has been constructed with appropriate and relevant questions. Additionally, a lot of care must be taken when identifying, screening, inviting prospects to participate in the focus groups. As a key principle, it is essential to clearly define the purpose of your focus group and the aim of the study. After securing consent from those selected to participate, it is advisable to offer them the option to withdraw at any time. The point here being, it is important to maintain trust.

As a final point, it is important to know that a moderator with high EQ knows how to transcend barriers. Enough for now. Let us stop here and roll the tape back in time.

8

Big Data Essentials: When Data Becomes as Prevalent as our Breath

"We are generating data at every move and with every breath. This means that while we are eating, driving, and generally living our life, our data footprint continues to grow. To be sure, data is definitely as prevalent as our breath yet, we all differ in how we generate it."

—Journel Joseph

Big data is not hype. It is actually real and has already transformed how we live and how companies and governments operate. The depth of data continues to grow at an astronomical pace at every second. To put this into context, consider the fact that more than **2.5 exabytes** (2.5 quintillion bytes), of data has been created every day[97] as of 2012. I will decode the magnitude of this statement in this chapter. It is important to highlight however, that 80 percent of the data generated is unstructured[98] (consisting of social media posts, photos, video and audio streaming, emails, reviews, documents, and more). Generally speaking, unstructured data contains critical information with high value, but is also ambiguous, unorganized and mired in irregularities. This makes it extremely difficult to process and prepare for analysis. In contrast, structured data is presented in an organized format and is easy to access, search and analyze. The trend has continued at an even faster pace since 2012 as we embarked on sweeping digital transformations. It is staggering and almost impossible to stay abreast with the proliferation of the quantity of data despite all the advances in big data solution technology. Considering the vast amount of data available for business decisions, "only 1 percent" of digital data has been analyzed, according to a 2016 McKinsey article. As the authors put it, "Often, those analyses are conducted as discrete one-offs—nifty experiments, but not much more. Indeed, in many companies, analytics initiatives still seem more like sideline science-fair projects than the core of a cutting-edge business model."[99] This leaves remarkable areas of opportunity to discover breakthroughs, deploy new products and services that are largely untapped. In the meantime, we are constantly generating a trail of activity which is being captured through our smartphones, censors, apps, facial recognition technology, IoTs, smart home assistant devices, at work and on the go. In short, we are generating data at every move and with every breath.

First Off, What Exactly Is Big Data?

There are a multitude of captivating definitions of big data. I will focus on a few of them here to demonstrate its constant and rapid evolution over the years. I will also explore and summarize several different scenarios. According to the *MIT Technology Review*, in 2001, "a Meta (now Gartner,)" report "noted the increasing size of data..." and "proposed a three-fold definition encompassing the three Vs: Volume, Velocity and Variety. This idea has since become popular and sometimes includes a fourth V, namely veracity, to cover questions of trust and uncertainty."[100] In 2011, McKinsey defined Big Data as "A growing torrent... flowing in every area of the global economy." In 2016, McKinsey added that "The revolution in big data analytics is starting to transform how companies organized, operated, managed talent and created value."[101] To conclude our exploration, Ernst & Young (EY) summarizes it perfectly: "Big data refers to the dynamic, large and disparate volumes of data being created by people, tools and machines. It requires new innovative and scalable technology to collect, host and analytically process the vast amount of data gathered in order to derive real-time business insights..."[102] Now that you have a brief idea of what big data entails, let us assess the following question: *What is your Data Footprint?*

Click, Swipe, Snap

To understand your contribution to big data, consider when you buy a smartphone or any electronic gadget, it comes with an amount of storage that varies in size (a smartphone for example, comes in 16GB to 512GB as discussed in chapter One.) As you use your home devices daily—Fitbits, smartphones, smartwatches, and open and navigate through Google Maps, Amazon Prime, Facebook, Instagram, Snapchat or YouTube apps—you are generating an undefined amount of data that is slowly filling up the storage of your device. Companies are vying to access your behavioral data; they need and develop tools to track your activities to understand your interests in order to know what to offer you in real-time. The data if not properly secured becomes appealing to cyber theft which creates serious data protection and privacy issues. We discuss this topic in the subsequent chapters and there will be more on the footprint of your data later. For now, let us take a look at the road traveled over the past few decades.

A Time in Space

In this respect, we need to step back and reflect on how far we have come to being contributors to big data on a daily basis. According to the National Aeronautics and Space Administration (NASA) your smartphone has more computing power than the original spacecraft Voyager 1 and 2 which was launched in 1977[103] and over the past 4 decades, they are still exploring the orbit where nothing from Earth has ever flown before. According to NASA, "Voyager 1 and Voyager 2 had 69.63 kilobytes of memory each. For comparison, an iPhone 5 with 16 gigabytes of memory has about 240,000 times the memory of a Voyager spacecraft."[104] Some of us would probably not be able to function with 16 gigabytes of memory anymore. I managed to painfully do so for about 2 years with my iPhone 6. I was able to keep only a few apps and maximize my iCloud usage by constantly switching (removing and replacing,) my apps as needed on my iPhone. I successfully kept that process up until I figured out that it was unproductive for my work. I initiated a great deal of my research on my iPhone; wrote hundreds of notes, used it for countless hours of reading, listened to Podcasts, streaming services (music, videos, courses,) and performed work activities and more. Clearly, I needed to upgrade my storage and doing so would also significantly increase my data footprint. Our smartphones, devices and insatiable appetite for capturing our most cherished memories (photos and videos), our dependency on various apps for our daily needs in addition to streaming movies and videos, saving and reading articles, and constantly interacting with friends on social media platforms are the drivers of big data creation. According to a Salesforce e-book entitled the *Rise of Systems of Intelligence,* social media constitutes for "the single largest data streams that are being created at astronomical volumes."[105]

Sit Tight

In this chapter, I will bring some clarity to this very complex topic which has consumed and revolutionized the business and government sectors. It is vital to have a clear understanding as we cruise into digitalization and interconnected systems. Having a clear understanding of the storage capacity of all the apps and content that you store in your smart devices (phones, watches, cars, tablets, computers, digital assistants, etc.) will enable you to process what big data constitutes and your role in it. They (the apps) collect and store our data as previously discussed, vary from work and personal emails to books, documents, notes, news and a wide-range of applications such as LinkedIn, Twitter, Facebook, Google, Netflix, YouTube, Amazon, Bible, Spotify, Lyft, Uber, Starbucks, Whatsapp, dating apps, Maps, Weather, Podcasts – the list is endless. All of these apps serve as gateways that produce a vast amount of data—thus the continuous tsunami of information begins generating right from our smart devices. When we consider the data collectively, we are all contributing in real-time and playing a substantial part in big data as previously indicated. There is no indication that we will be stopping any time soon. That considered, let us get back to the question. Try to reflect on how big your data input is for just a moment. How wide is your data footprint? It is probably very hard or almost impossible to measure or quantify, right? Keep in mind that as long as you wake up, pick up your phone, turn on your smart devices, go to work, call or text a friend, take a walk or fall asleep, you are continuously generating data. This means that while you are eating, driving, and generally living your life, your data footprint continues to grow. To be sure, data is definitely as prevalent as our breath yet, we all differ in how we generate it.

Understanding the Magnitude of Big Data

Let us explore the magnitude of big data. At this point, you are probably starting to have a sense of the sheer amount of data being produced. Considering your personal data input is a good start, but know that it is invisible in the ocean of big data. Let us go back to the amount of data I indicated was being created on a daily basis—over 2.5 quintillion bytes (2.5 exabytes). This is probably no longer a surprise and I hope you are getting the big picture. Allow me to break this down in the very simplest form. When you go and purchase a smartphone, you probably check on its capacity, and know that the storage size of the phone dictates the price. The storage size in our electronic gadgets is measured in bytes. One byte is equivalent to a grouping of 8 bits, or a single "typed character" or letter.[106] A bit is considered as the smallest unit of storage in the world of digital communication and computing. It is fairly certain that you are familiar with terms such as kilobytes, megabytes and gigabytes as it pertains to the usage of the storage space in your smartphone. The balance of the size of your data footprint depends on the type of device you are using and how much content you have stored by interacting with the apps that you download as well as those that actually come with the phone. As you manage the usage on the device, you can free up space or optimize your storage by deleting or storing the content on the cloud. An easy and quick tip is to offload unused apps when you are low on storage. This basically constitutes some of the options you have that you probably rarely use. Companies heavily rely on the data we produce to inform their decisions from designing new products, planning and executing targeted marketing campaigns and improving user experience.

Beyond our individual data input as an example, consider that in 2017, there were over 65 billion messages shared on the WhatsApp app daily and 2 billion minutes of private voice and video calls made every day during the year.[107] Google handled over 50,000 queries per second on average, according to the Internet Live Stats.[108] Compare these staggering figures to 1998, when Google processed less than 10,000 searches per day, and by 2004 "users were submitting over 200 million" search queries daily to Google. While big data is very complex, it is most certainly not an abstract notion. The goal is to help you process and visualize the sheer magnitude of your data footprint, and our collective contribution to big data daily.

Decoding the Daily Production of Big Data

One exabyte equals one quintillion (one thousand quadrillion) bytes—that is 1 + 18 zeros (1,000,000,000,000,000,000). Indiana University describes an exabyte as the equivalent of "212,765,958 single-sided DVDs (a stack that's about 255.3 kilometers, or 158.65 miles, tall)."[109] These measures could still be intimidating or even overwhelming to wrap your head around. The number 2.5 exabytes equals 2.5 billion (2,500,000,000) gigabytes of data. Let us try and put this into a broader and practical perspective.

Now, envision giving a smartphone with the capacity of 16GB completely filled with data to every single inhabitant of France with 67.11 million, Canada with 36.70 million, Columbia with 49.06 million and Ireland 4.81 million.[110] If we are to combine all of these numbers, the sample population will amount to more than 157,000,000 people, which is nearly half of the population of the U.S. Imagine all of these people with their smartphones jam-packed to the point where they cannot even operate the device to take a picture or send a text message without freeing up space (157,000,000 x 16, totaling to over 2.5 billion gigabytes or over 2.5 exabytes). This should give you a better idea of the daily production of data and much more.

Everlasting Pursuit

A 2017 Pew Research Center survey reported that in the United States alone about 77 percent of adults own a smartphone and 59 percent say they use their phones to shop online, while another 55 percent indicate that "They get news alerts on their phones."[111] According to the World Economic Forum and Statista (a leading provider of market and consumer data,) there are approximately 2.5 billion of smartphone users,[112] around the world in 2018 and "This figure is predicted to rise to almost three (3) billion by 2020."[113] We do not even need to figure out the outcome of these figures. We are being inundated with big data and there are even more users as we enter the interconnected systems and smart cities. From what we have seen in the above paragraphs, the core challenge is that enterprises have still not grasped how to gain valuable intelligence from big data.

Big Data in the Age of the Supercomputer

Advancements in computing power continue to move beyond the realm of human imagination. This picture was further corroborated with the announcement of the "Summit" in June 2018. Being labeled as the world's fastest computer, it has the capacity to process 200,000 trillion calculations per second.[114] With that amount of speed, the United States became number one and overtook China's dominance to regain the world's most powerful computer. The *NY Times* estimates that the tasks performed by Summit—supported by artificial intelligence would take a human 6.3 billion years to perform.[115] Additionally, according to the *MIT Technology Review*, it is "The first supercomputer designed from the ground up to handle machine learning, neural networks and other AI applications."[116] The race to control supercomputers is growing at lightning speed and the aim is to use the Summit as the stepping stone. The *MIT Technology Review* further asserts that "Topping the supercomputing charts isn't just a matter of national pride. The machines are widely used in industry and also for national security tasks, such as developing nuclear weapons. Lessons from Summit will also inform the push to create "exascale" computers capable of handling a billion billion calculations a second. These are expected to come online in the early 2020s."[117]

The Next Frontier: Prevalence of Big Data in Today's Machine Age

The immense quantity of data being created will continue to increase exponentially as we interact and enter an interconnected world. Consider all that the rise of systems of intelligence will bring to our lives from Internet of Things (IoTs), autonomous vehicles, sensors, smart cameras, 5G technology, smart cities and the billions of gadgets that are generating data. According to McKinsey "By 2020, some 50 billion smart devices will be connected, along with billions of additional smart sensors, ensuring that the global supply of data will continue to more than double every two years."[118] With such a vast amount of data being generated daily—only intelligent machines will have the capability to gather, crunch and fully gain insights from big data. This will probably lead to new discoveries in medicine in ways we cannot even imagine. It will be immensely valuable to our future by significantly augmenting human abilities and will eventually transform and create new paradigms to every single industry. As we move forward, the ability of analysts and managers to interact with machines and develop confidence in them will be crucial in optimizing the possibilities of big data. Corporations are more prone than ever to embracing advanced analytics that unearth valuable insights. They are still however, struggling to develop a comprehensive and holistic data strategy. Moving along with the rise of automation to gather and analyze data and deliver real-time data-driven decisions remains the utmost challenge for businesses. This does not suggest that the ball is not moving. The best companies are indeed pushing the envelope to generate more accurate forecasts in addition to setting their business modules on the path to success. That said, securing the data remains a constant challenge for companies and government agencies and we are facing new kinds of security threats and risks daily that can alter the course of our society.

The Digital Warfare

On the Ground: The Emerging Risks That Challenge Human Nature

The information warfare is happening, and this is not only featured in an episode from the hit show *Homeland* on HBO. It is real in our modern day's age of big data and requires companies and governments to develop concerted and coordinated campaigns and take a broad view approach that goes beyond their immediate boundaries. It is crucial to focus on the structural challenges of a maligned influence and the disinformation that seems endemic to social media platforms,[119] such as Twitter, Facebook, Instagram, WhatsApp and YouTube. The problem cannot be viewed in isolation rather, it must fit into the adoption of a broader threat of intelligence initiatives. Current solutions seem to do little to mitigate the threat and companies continue to play catch up while the offenders remain 2 steps ahead. It is only a matter of time before this practice becomes fully automated with AI-powered systems since it can also be trained to produce false information and manages to trick users into believing falsehoods as accuracy. The present practice is to use AI to detect and combat falsehoods, and the threat actors are using similar technology to advance their cause—which is shaping to eventually become a race to nowhere if the trend continues in its current form. Consider that a cyber-attack can be managed or contained even in its aftermath, and is more devastating for our society than has been reported thus far. Further, it primarily targets the physical and materialistic aspects of our society. High-profiled organizations such as Target, Equifax and Sony have all been impacted by cyber-attacks and have managed to clean and recuperate some of their data assets. If we are to consider that the fake data that is being disseminated on social media platforms is targeting our cognitive functions as well as our belief systems, behaviors and our well-being, it is safe to say that it poses serious threats to our world at large. If we fail to solve this critical issue by making it our primary responsibility and drastically reassess how we address this existential threat, it could significantly alter our lives and probably already has. When adding cyber to the information warfare which could change how customers perceive your organization at every click, the impact could be irreparable. This should never be about "*them versus us,*"—the protection of fundamental human rights is at risk.

So, It is Complicated! Information Warfare in the Age of Big Data: An Evolving Threat

The upsurge of foreign actors targeting the communication systems of citizens from other countries is defined as information warfare and has reached a new frontier. This can easily be assessed through recent events in the United States and Europe. It refers to the coordinated information operations performed by foreign actors to disrupt and create distrust in established systems. Again, this is not an episode of the hit shows *Homeland* or *Person of Interest* where there is a machine that sees and detects everything. That is to say these are real-life occurrences and these practices have already targeted and reached citizens in various countries including the United States, France during the period leading to the 2016 and 2017 elections and in Great Britain during the Brexit referendum as recounted by various news media and investigative reports.[120] Such threats present serious national security risks and could significantly disrupt governments and businesses in counties that are becoming heavily dependent on interconnected digital infrastructure. The malicious actors have taken advantage of big data and the vulnerabilities of open societies to inject their political discourse with disinformation and "fake news." These threats have had a broad impact on social media platforms, considering the various reports of questionable content generated by fake bots, burner accounts, and impostors. They use the flaws in these social media sites to flood users with contentious and compromised information.

The High Stakes

The information warfare is being waged on social media where the risk is growing intensely. This is particularly terrifying as AI-generated fake videos (deep fakes) are prone to being exploited. Evidently, information warfare is a real thing and extremely complex. We are now seeing the emergence of a new kind of threat actor that targets the United States and the democratic foundations of other countries, the reputations of their businesses, their population, and their belief systems. They have weaponized information and targeted the most vulnerable of these societies by using social media platforms which have become the gateway and the heart of the communication systems of western countries. Current efforts and strategies to contain the danger reveal how challenging it has become to purge complex internet platforms from questionable data. The process remains largely fragmented and inefficient to this point. This may well be the tip of the iceberg as we move deeper into digitalization. If not properly addressed, this could lead to collective fear, frustration and destructive outcomes for the world.

Okay, So Now What Is Next?

It depends. Frankly, at this point, there are no viable solutions to contain these cyber threats, and the digital warfare—and that is the current reality. I will share some ideas to explore in this chapter in addition to subsequent ones. As we move forward, we must take a holistic approach and consider taking proactive actions that are not in isolation, but apply to organizations that respond to such risks more broadly and collaboratively. Further, it is important to leverage technology to purge disreputable content or establish rigorous processes to make sure data is not used to cause reputational harm, or violate the privacy of citizens.

Spotting the Sources

Respectable organizations must build their credibility by ensuring that strong data quality protocols are in place and include processes to detect, authenticate and certify all originators of content—let us refer to them as "sources." This could be a company, political party, government agency, bots, an influencer or individual. What do I mean? Consider that I cite over 150 sources in this book. Now, take for example Fortune, which I reference several times, but in different subjects, topics or publications. Fortune is the original source, but subjects as accounts can be easily changed. AI-powered bots could be trained to create fake accounts and content, and disguise themselves from one social media platform to another. The intent here is to track behaviors of sources that could be displayed and detected as trends, outliers, or patterns as we discussed in the TOP techniques. It would require more in-depth, sophisticated and costly strategies to repeatedly change sources, yet they would be contained and tracked. Additionally, all social media platforms must require satirical content to be labeled with a warning. In chapter 11, I discuss the complexity and enormity of the challenge for a tech giant such as Facebook to police over 1.4 billion daily active users on its platform in the manner it is currently being done. I want to emphasize that we must follow and verify creators or sources of data beyond the content that is being generated for individual accounts. This will require building partnerships between social media platforms and internet providers for a more robust strategy. This could serve as the baseline to build upon. Such a tactic would likely aid to design technology solutions with the capability to detect trends, outliers and patterns in content generations from data sources. Imagine how this approach would assist in identifying posts or tweets from automated accounts, assess whether there are consistent patterns or identify emerging trends from specific sources and geographic locations. We must take a holistic approach by aiming to understand the intricacies of this evolving type of threat to our society and develop ways to contain it.

Beware: With Big Data Comes Big Risk

As previously indicated, with over 2.5 quintillion bytes or 2.5 billion gigabytes of data created every day, you may have heard the dictum *"garbage in, garbage out."* Developing a strategy to contain questionable content that is easily accessible with a smartphone and where anyone can create a narrative that can go viral via social media is a daunting task. Dealing with the growing number of deceptive posts, videos, photos, and tweets would require a more in-depth and elaborate strategy that goes beyond a company's constant obsession for views, click-through rates, likes and page popularity.

Deleting impersonated or dubious bot accounts and not solely the content, would be a good business decision not only to inspire trust, but to save companies from infrastructure and expenditure costs. By being vigilant about removing harmful content and accounts, they would be freeing up storage space on their cloud server farms and improving their digital ecosystems. Make no mistake, any holistic and effective action that deals with a significant amount of fake data flowing into digital platforms requires partnerships or alliances between internet providers and social media companies to ensure that the perpetrators are held liable. These threats are serious, and pose destructive and dangerous threats towards the business environment. They must be dealt with rigor rather than the usual *"3 strikes you are out"* type of approach.

Contaminated Content Hidden in the Fast Lane of Social Media

This is an even more dangerous issue as social media platforms have let the door open to blur the lines between freedom of speech, satirical conspiracy and unsavory content. There should be a banner or *warning label* that clearly indicates that the content about to be viewed is bad satire out of respect for those who are reading or watching and for those who are being portrayed in those fake videos or photos. They owe their users and society that much. It is a simple matter of ethical responsibility to establish code of conduct and principles to remove or ban non-compliant sources. The process should be similar to the requirements for drug companies to carry warnings on their medications. As a result, broadcasted (TV, radio, telephone) prescription drug or product claim advertisements are mandated to disclose the side effects of the drugs and non-compliance could have severe consequences. The idea is not to prevent or deny free speech, but rather providing targeted users with a choice and a clear understanding of the risks involved—eventually society will develop an immune response to them. Social media platforms that leave them unclassified, or unpunished when violated are as responsible as the deceitful content creators. How far this will advance in today's age of ultra-fast digitalization where a significant portion of the population does not authenticate information, is yet to be determined. The matter is very complicated.

To conclude this section, I want to stress that the trolls, bots or impersonated accounts began as outliers to test reactions, then evolved into an emerging trend. This is probably where we are now. How to reverse or contain the trend is the key question that must consume the minds of technology companies as well as their executives and board of directors.

Harvesting Data in the Age of Big data: Pilot, Test, Validate and Augment

"On average, less than 50 percent of structured data is used in making decisions—and less than 1 percent of an organization's unstructured data is analyzed or used at all. More than 70 percent of employees have access to data they should not, and 80 percent of analysts' time is spent simply discovering and preparing data."[121]
—Thomas H. Davenport

Given the unprecedented quantities of data available as indicated countless times in this book, harvesting accurate, reliable and relevant data for your analytics projects could be a serious undertaking. Considering that 80 percent of an analyst's time is spent preparing and cleaning data according to the *Harvard Business Review*,[122] companies can succeed or fail depending on how they handle the data available to them. Fraudulent, fake or biased data could damage the reputation of enterprises and cause serious trust issues amongst its patrons. One way to avoid such pitfalls to propagate further into the digital pipeline of your company is to consider a more simplified process. There is a certain amount of data that any project will need to be operational and this explains why sampling methods exist, as previously discussed. This approach would require that you initially focus on practical, manageable and testable steps. This would also require you to consider piloting your data collection project on a manageable scale in order to create an underlying theoretical framework and proof of concepts. The methods for this framework would need to be replicable. The next step would be to develop a model; synthesize, validate and filter the data. Select and focus on the key indicators and the phenomenon that you want to investigate. During the course of the process, it is essential to use sampling schemes to standardize the results and capture the essence of the data to predict some outcomes and inform critical business decisions as you move forward. Whether you are reinventing or using advanced analytics systems for your projects or building a whole new ecosystem from scratch, it is critical to determine how fast the system is able to adjust in real-time, as discussed in chapter 4. This will be essential to optimizing performances in a very complex and wild business landscape.

Course Correction: Focus on What Matters

By using the pilot first, you are offered a unique opportunity to learn, clean up your data, course correct—extrapolate and augment. This approach is vital to helping develop a proof of concept for your data and analytics initiatives—before you prioritize, test and validate your results. It is important to move forward with a tested proof of concept that is supported by a well-documented explanation of every critical juncture in your journey. Taking the essential step to pilot can enable you to become strategic and define how to scale up as part of the process to build an agile organization that is apt to embrace change. As you move forward, you will have the opportunity to observe any potential shifts away from the baseline, investigate the cause, and course correct. Adopting the method of piloting and testing will give your team the ability to learn, iterate, respond to complexities such as changing conditions, uncertainties and ensuring that data architecture systems and technologies are built to adapt and adjust accordingly.

Advances come with new challenges. Before considering this notion, it is worth asking a fundamental question. *How do you focus on what matters to gain the most relevant insights?* You have to ensure that the system is viable before it takes control of itself. This is vital to avoid a structural problem that could be hard to reverse in the age of automation. That said, I want to underline that testing or pushing the boundaries are necessary to overcome challenges, expand the mark and discover new opportunities, but knowing when to stop is probably the biggest obstacle. No matter how fast or powerful supercomputers and technology solutions are being designed, the data quality will *always* define the findings.

PART FOUR

AUTOMATED SYSTEMS, DATA PROTECTION AND PRIVACY PARADOX

9

The Next Frontier: Data Collection in the Modern Day's Age of Automation

"The fear about the future of companies and their staff is centered around the unknown role that artificial intelligence will play in the future of work. What has always remained uncertain is the right proportion and balance of human + machine to build an efficient workforce. That should keep all executives awake at night."

—Journel Joseph

We are entering the next frontier of data collection which is driven by automation and creates limitless opportunities as well as numerous challenges. Data automation techniques combined with advanced cognitive computing are progressively being used by data scientists, researchers, artificial intelligence and machine learning professionals. Turning big data into insights will have a profound impact on how companies make decisions and operate. As a result, making data a primary asset is indisputably vital for an organization's survival. This is particularly essential considering the proliferation of smart sensors, apps, Internet of Things (IoTs), intelligent voice-driven devices, the prevalence of facial recognition technology, imagery captured by sophisticated satellites and unarmed aerial vehicles (UAVs) which are commonly known as drones. They will all work in synchronization to generate massive quantities of data as users, customers or individuals interact with them. These smart devices and applications that have the ability to generate large amounts of data are powered by machine learning and artificial intelligence technologies. To be certain, they are prone to lead the fundamental changes in data collection methods. According to a survey conducted by NPR and Edison Research "One in Six Americans" have a smart speaker like Amazon Echo, Google Home, Microsoft Cortana, Apple HomePod, or Sonos One—and 65 percent indicated that they "Would not go back to a life without one."[123] This is just the beginning as more AI-powered devices move into our homes, cars, work environments and smart cities. Ericsson forecasts that by the year 2020, there will be "Around 29 billion connected devices, of which around 18 billion will be related to IoTs."[124] This is driving companies to an unsettling quest to what Patrick McGinnis describes as "FOMO" (Fear of Missing Out). The numbers raise the most important question to be determined as we build the future: *How will we protect the privacy of customers during the process of this rapid race towards automation and interconnected systems?*

"Every part of our lives, our homes, our cars, our workplaces, our factories and cities — every sector of our economy, whether it's precision

agriculture, precision medicine, autonomous cars or autonomous drones, personalized medicine or personalized banking — are all being transformed by digital technology." —Satya Nadella[125]

Robotic Process Automation (RPA)

Unlike anything we have experienced previously, RPA is rapidly changing the paradigm of automation. It is driving the transformation within various industries, including accounting and finance, healthcare, energy, agriculture, transportation, research far beyond what we could have imagined just few years ago. KPMG describes RPA as a "game-changing technology." And argues "Using RPA to automate transactional activities improves accuracy, efficiency, and speed of critical business processes while also freeing up people to focus on more strategic work and driving greater job satisfaction."[126] KPMG cautions that implementing RPA in your business operations should not be a wild chase—it argues "Its adaptation across the enterprise can be explosive and disjointed, with business units acting on their own without governance and oversight."[127] Therefore, it is important to build a centralized ecosystem to control and manage its deployment—and balance the need for speed with the need for control, according to KPMG.

During an interview conducted by Xavier Lhuer, Associate Principal at McKinsey—Leslie Willcocks, professor of technology at the London School of Economics—provides a comprehensive framework to understand and categorize RPA, explaining "There are four streams of RPA. The first is a highly customized software that will work only with certain types of process in, say, accounting and finance." He describes "The more general streams, in terms of a three-lane motorway. The slow lane is what we call screen scraping or web scraping. A user might be collecting data, synthesizing it, and putting it into some sort of document on a desktop. You automate as much of that as possible." Further, Willcocks adds, "The second lane in terms of power is a self-development kit where a template is provided and specialist programmers design the robot. That's usually customized for a specific organization. The fast lane is enterprise/enterprise-safe software that can be scaled and is reusable."[128]

The need to automate administrative and labor intensive tasks has always been one of the primary goals of advances in technology over the years. As a result, the application of automation technologies, robotic process automation (RPA) has emerged as the breakthrough that can imitate a human brain to perform repetitive tasks at a much higher level. RPA has broad applications—it goes beyond and is much more in-depth than merely screen or web scraping, which is considered as one of its basic functions, as previously described. Though applying Robotic Process Automation (RPA) will provide a high level of speed and efficiency, data quality and privacy risks must be seriously taken into consideration.

The Scrapers

Collecting data through what we commonly refer to as web scraping has become common practice. Simply put, this entails automating collection of online data by using computer software techniques (codes, bots or scripts). The method is rapidly becoming more and more invasive as our daily lives, the web and social network platforms become inundated with data. To put this term into perspective, consider the "copy and paste" technique which is frequently used. By identifying something you like and duplicating it via copy and paste rather than retyping it repeatedly, you can accomplish the task quickly and efficiently. This process in simple terms can be referred to as the human version of scraping. Screen or web scraping is a more efficient way of processing and performing the task of harvesting vast amounts of data by automating the practice. There are varied tools available for web scraping which include Python, R, JavaScript and Ruby on Rails that are each equipped with libraries to scrape data in a fast and efficient way. I want to underline that these techniques bring significant data privacy risk—yet, serve as valuable skillset for a data scientist toolbox. Recent data misuse events have put data privacy (long ignored) in the forefront—it helps to explore the applications, potential impacts and some of the risks that come with implementing these automated data collection techniques.

Foundational Breakdowns: At the Core of Automated Data Collection

Traditionally, conducting any type of research study involved a lengthy planning process that was essential for developing a study protocol, reliable and relevant instruments (surveys, interview and focus group guides,) and requesting permission from the Institutional Review Board (IRB). This would be followed by a long wait until the approval was granted in order to proceed. However, various reputable organizations, government agencies and academic institutions are still actively using conventional and scientifically tested and proven methods to collect data. The evolution of data gathering offers a valuable opportunity to take advantage of the fast-changing pace of digitalization as well as the new technology that was once too speculative, hazy (or unreliable) to embrace.

Things are rapidly changing, but adopting code of ethics to these new automated methods of data collection and analytics remains a challenge. What is clear, is that automation offers you the opportunity to innovate, harvest massive amounts of data and extract hidden values in a virtual and controlled environment.

Once you have secured the data, you can proceed in performing a series of tasks ranging from cleansing, to analyzing, to drawing inferences. In some cases, the data is used to train artificial intelligence or machine learning models. Currently, this is being executed in a manner that was probably inconceivable just a few years ago. I would like to stress that conventional methods such as surveys, interviews and focus groups will continue to remain key drivers in data collection—and could be valuable particularly in validating unstructured data that has been collected through automated techniques (as discussed in the scenario in chapter 6). Notwithstanding, technology offers innovative ways to automate some components of these traditional data collection methods. It will enable you to connect, screen, communicate and follow up with a large sample size of customers in a fast paced and affordable way.

Data Collection: The Dawn of a New Day

Data Comes with Responsibility

Social media platforms are being used as the gateway to collect data to understand the behaviors and interests of users. Polls are being conducted on Twitter to acquire the sentiments on a myriad of issues from participants who tweet, and it is being done in real-time. The findings are critical and can be used to help influence business decisions. To ensure the protection and privacy of the data collected, these platforms can secure consent *prior* to taking the surveys and polls and require that all apps collecting data to disclose how it will be used. This will work as a sort of check and balance and empower the users by requiring their approval beforehand. Using data to target customers is the new normal and will not change, but it absolutely can and must be done the right way. This is the simple fact of the digital age. Customers are awakening to what is at stake and need and expect their data to be protected. The process will also require that the advertising pricing models for example, are modified, while providing more value to the company, the users and the advertisers.

Historically, the abuse and misuse of data through constant tracking is what amounts to conducting surveillance unbeknownst to individuals. This practice has been used for decades and results in countless disasters and atrocities. While once denounced when the government used it—it has become commonplace in today's business model. The perception that the government or a company could be tracking your every move could be considered invasive and lead to an eventual revolt by consumers. On the contrary, these sorts of practices impede progress and create a hesitance in adopting new technology. As a result, lifesaving and transformative discoveries such as personalized medicine become derailed. It is more of a disadvantage for a company to continue on a careless path of personal data misuse. Every enterprise that is serious about the future beyond short-term gain should intensify their efforts towards data privacy and put their resources towards the advancement of protecting personal information. This is the only path toward remaining relevant and competitive.

What Do the Changes in Data Gathering Mean for Scientific Research Methods?

An article published in 1983, titled *A Comparison of Automated Data Collection and Manual Data Collection for Toxicology Studies*, found "Online data collection increases the quality of the data gathered because: 1) it facilitates scientific observation by displaying historical data and statistics on changes since the last observation period; 2) it virtually eliminates errors due to oversight and transcription; 3) it allows more careful monitoring of the course of the study by providing immediate access to interim summary statistics; 4) it provides complete documentation of all changes made to the data after initial collection. In addition, automated data collection enables more rapid completion of the final report of results…"[129] Evidently, automated data collection has been tested, proven and refined over past decades—it is not new. What has changed?

The sheer volume, variety, velocity and veracity of data generated through social networks, sensors, facial recognition technology, smart devices on a daily basis presents both opportunities (the ability to compile and combine data from multiple sources at a low cost), and challenges (requires technical expertise to aggregate data, privacy consideration, validity checks, and quality control issues). As a 2017 Deloitte article puts it, "Society and businesses have fallen in love with big data. We can't get enough: The more we collect, the more we want. Some companies hoard data, unsure of its value or unclear if or when it will be useful to them…"[130]

It is important to be clear that not all data is created equal. The main challenge becomes how to select the relevant and accurate data from all the noise that comes with big data.

The disturbing fact to consider is that some of the abusive methods used in data gathering are done in excess. Would the act of vacuuming all of the moves, posts, and activities of every user really lead to more valuable or reliable insights? It is highly unlikely that data overload without context will yield significant insight. The point here is that gathering data without proper context may not necessarily be better for your analytics project. In addition, it is a challenging task to detect and remove dubious and disparate data that has been generated by fake bot accounts. Perhaps we need to reevaluate how we process big data and be more methodological in our approach. I would recommend as previously mentioned in chapter 7, to consider piloting the use of data based on sampling methods. This will help to build strong proof of concepts that are supported by practical applications.

Keeping Order

In reality, research methods such as sampling schemes have been used for several decades. With an astonishing level of confidence, inferences are made about populations based solely on data that has been gathered from sampling methods. If a sample is selected from a particular demographic group, the findings would be applicable to that specific group only. These techniques are still being used in scientific research to demonstrate the correlation, and the cause and effect (respectively in observational and experimental studies), and in varied industries including clinical trials for medical discoveries or therapy. The widely used observational study, for example, has its limitations due to confounding factors. This is where advances in analytical tools with the computing power to process large amounts of data could serve as a reinforcement for those types of studies and aid in addressing potential flaws. Keep in mind, as repeatedly discussed in this book, the findings will only be as good as the quality of the data used—regardless of its size.

Data Quality Matters

Processing large amounts of data is no longer a challenge, but the quality of the data is the hot-button issue. Given the ever-present threat of contaminated data, companies must take drastic action to streamline the quality of data that is being fed through their pipeline or AI systems. This refers to the trust and uncertainty that depicts the veracity of big data as discussed at the beginning of this chapter. According to IMB "Poor data quality costs the U.S. economy around $3.1 trillion a year."[131] Evidently, ignoring the effects of contagious and fraudulent data has led to costly and irreparable damage. Having embarked on this difficult path to survive and remain viable, organizations must understand the risks and responsibilities associated with big data.

Data can equate to the flow of a stream of water that is rushing into a lake. Pollutants that were once blending in the stream will be carried along into the lake and to other locations where they will remain continuously buried. They dissolve in the lake and become consumed by plants and fish before being passed on to humans. Eventually, it will lead to a potential epidemic. Similar to unsavory data, by the time this crisis has been discovered, it would be close to impossible to contain. A good example would be an AI-infused system that has been tainted and trained with fake data. It would generate dubious insights and eventually become disruptive to humanity. We simply cannot afford to neglect contaminated data as we progress towards interconnected systems with big data and

AI at the center of their transformation. It is important to develop systems that will detect the sources of data pollutants and cut them off at their point of entry. The solution to contaminated data is complex, but the first step is to eliminate the toxins that are infecting the content at its source. If already infected, it is important to treat the data before using it in order to avoid costly and irreparable damage. Appropriate quality control procedures and data management systems combined with effective measures for privacy and protection are essential.

It All Happens So Fast! How Did We Get Here?

Due to the advancement of technology today, we certainly cannot return to the outdated and painfully slow methods of data gathering in today's age of big data. That said, we must proceed with the utmost caution. Advances in technology and computing power provide breakthroughs and ways to improve data collection. They also have the ability to expand the boundaries beyond what was previously unimaginable—in the process, the need for privacy has been lost.

Beware

The race to predict who is going to obtain the largest amount of data seems to be superficially advancing on the surface while ignoring the legitimate concerns that are related to data quality. The point here is taking extreme lengths to make inferences based on the interests, habits and even political tendencies of customers (while ignoring data privacy) is unwise. Data that has been overloaded and misused could slacken or even bias your business models to draw irrelevant conclusions on your specific market segment. For a more accurate outcome, a deep cleansing by using advanced technology and skilled analysts, as well as additional data from reliable sources would be required to ensure that you are making decisions that are based on the most relevant insights.

Over the past few years, technology company startups have promoted their abilities to build robust models by using hundreds or thousands of data points that they have scrapped from social media users. The methods have grown and evolved by using advanced analytic techniques to model an individual's behavior and predict their needs in real-time. While this may sound amazing, consider that your privacy may be in jeopardy!

A 2017 report by the Digital Planet, Tufts University summarizes and provides a thorough context to understand the challenges related to data privacy and digital trust, *"As technology improves, more complexity is being embedded into algorithms resulting in consumers' data being used in ways that are not fully understood by consumers themselves. This opacity can also create questions about the trustworthiness of what happens behind the scenes, how the increasingly powerful digital players are using the information, and whether privacy, security and accuracy are being maintained as consumers' reliance on digital technologies grows."*[132]

Erosion of Privacy: What Can Go Wrong?

The unsuspecting users of social media platforms are compromising all of their personal information on a daily basis—often trick into giving access to their data without consent—by taking quizzes or using game apps. As you enter your information on these third-party applications, you are also granting them access to your profile and recent privacy events suggest that these actions will eventually result in grave predicaments. Very few of the respondents that are taking those quizzes actually know what they are signing up for when they click on those sites. They often use ingenious ways of attracting users via alluring and catchy titles and with just a few clicks, their personal data has been released. In the next chapter, I will discuss how companies must ensure that these kinds of tools for harvesting personal data are not violating the rights of their users. Such laissez-faire will lead to more stringent regulations, and large enforcement fines for violations of individual privacy rights.

A 2017 KPMG report identifies data privacy as one of the top 10 key regulatory challenges for 2018—driven by "Heightened public sensitivity to data privacy and data protection." In addition to "Evolving state, jurisdictional, and global privacy regulations and regulatory expectations."[133]

Be Aware of your Customer's Privacy

Most applications using automated techniques to collect data have yet to follow the most basic data protection and privacy protocols. A very simple example would be asking for consent, and ensuring that the data is masked and encrypted. In 2010, Steve Jobs, the visionary and co-founder of Apple, put it plainly during an interview with journalists Walt Mossberg and Kara Swisher. In response to a question about whether or not privacy was viewed differently in Silicon Valley than in other locations, he commented, "We have always had a very different view of privacy than some of our colleagues in the Valley." He explained that privacy was built in his company's DNA. He also stated that "Privacy meant that people knew what they were signing up for, in plain English. I believe that people are smart, and some people want to share more data than other people do. Ask them. Ask them every time. Make them tell you to stop asking them if they get tired of your asking them. Let them know precisely what you are going to do with their data."[134] This is important in the digital age where every click or like can lead to the disclosure of personal data or the interests and location of a user.

Social media interactions and posts are primarily optimized for maximum engagement. They are measured and promoted based on the popularity of views, likes, and clicks—regardless of being fake or real content. As technology companies such as Facebook, Twitter, YouTube and others secure the access to data collection by third parties—some will adopt newer measures to adapt even quicker in order to thrive and remain in business. Bad actors clearly understand how a convincing headline (clickbait) can entice a user to click, swipe—input his or her phone number, email address, or grant access to their accounts in exchange for information they consider to be valuable. In return, their data will be strategically collected and used for other means, such as ransomware or phishing—for example, hackers could use personal emails for phishing scams (deceiving messages but convincing or believable enough to get them to click on links that plant malware on their devices). Following a data breach, companies can reset passwords, or a customer can update his or her password, cancel bank and credit cards or get a new Driver's License or Social Security number if necessary—but you cannot really change who you are or personal information (date of birth, schools, gender, relatives, etc.) shared on your social media profile. Protecting personally identifiable information (PII) is a serious and depressing challenge for technology companies and governments to overcome in the digital era.

Beware: The Revenge of the Customers

The obsession of tracking your customer's way of life and constantly trolling their online behavior, interests, and locations in real-time could be considered as corporate digital stalking and is unhealthy for business innovations. Data protection and privacy regulations, such as the GDPR, are invalidating business models built on the premise that users will grant their consent as a trad-eoff for access to their personal and private information without consent. To survive and thrive in the digital age you must re-code your business model to make privacy a business imperative.

It is important to highlight that tech entrepreneurs are revolutionary rules breakers. They thrive to change the world and how it operates. They break boundaries in the process, and conceive some amazing advancements for society. However, there must be considerable caution, codes of conduct and ethics when dealing with the lives and well-being of human subjects. If the trend of data misuse continues, a potential customer revolt would redefine and completely alter how we interact and communicate on social media, the future of innovation and interconnected systems. Companies as a result, have the obligation to promote the best practices and ensure that data protection and privacy becomes the norm.

Do Not Mess Things Up for a Quick Win

It is definitely time to forgo the easy, fast and creepy methods and focus on using advances in technology, ethical guidelines and moral judgment to facilitate innovation, breakthroughs to make the world a better place. At this point, the population is riddled with fear as to what to expect from the future. It is understandable as some of the ideas being discussed sound like an episode of *Black Mirror* from Netflix—particularly from episode 1 of season 4. In a specific scene, a disturbed intern, Nanette Cole, finds herself in the *USS Callister* spaceship and tries to understand what has happened to her. She is transported into the cinematic, customized universe of the captain, Robert Daly, by having her DNA extracted from the lid of a coffee-cup—she is trapped along with virtual clones of her coworkers. The irony is the previous scenes show how Nanette admires the captain and feels privileged to work for him. Obsessed by the need for control of his own universe, he uses Nanette's DNA to create a digital avatar of her. She finds herself disoriented in a strange place and begins to question what has occurred while wondering if she is dreaming. Eventually, she is informed that she is stuck in the captain's playground. And she revolted. Similarly, if companies fail to act responsibly, they could eventually face a potential customer's revolt—as they feel trapped in what Walton describes to Nanette as "An eternal waking nightmare from which there is no escape."[135] Obviously, this is a dystopian TV show that went far beyond what is possible in real-life, but the important lesson here is to understand that excessive data misuse could be disruptive and generate fear that risk preventing customers from adopting and using your products.

My recommendation to business managers, executives, policy-makers and those who are designing and building the future, is to ensure that their customers adopt their products and services to improve their lives. It is the company's job to protect the rights of their customers, educate them, show them respect, and create ways to make them more comfortable without falling for deceptive tricks. Jeopardizing the integrity of a business practice for a quick win is simply not worth it. Always remember that humanity depends on the continued progress of technology.

Shaping the Way

General Protection Regulation: GDPR

The journey from over a decade ago to today's high-powered technological capabilities of gathering data, creates immense opportunities as well as challenges. That is to say, although we are in a better place, we must maintain strong ethical conduct and be conscientious of our responsibilities as we build the future. Ensuring data privacy is essential for capitalizing on the advanced computing tools that collect, process and analyze data in order to drive insights, innovate and remain competitive. The European General Data Protection Regulation (GDPR) is leading the way. The GDPR went into effect on May 25, 2018, and has changed the landscape of data privacy. Its impact will expand beyond the EU zone. Varied countries around the world are actively planning to develop their own regulations to protect their citizens. There are well over 100 countries around the world that have some level of data privacy policy. The enforcement mechanism and focus of the GDPR on governing the collection of personal data of EU citizens compels companies to obtain personal consent from their customers before accessing their individual data. It has been defined as personally identifiable information (PII) and must be handled and stored with the utmost care.

Insights Inside the GDPR

Data privacy is a life-long journey and should be a shared responsibility. Users, as well as organizations, should be responsible for adopting and following safe practices and policies—it cannot

Source: European Union
General Data Protection Regulation (GDPR)

be left to the companies alone. Since the policies requiring the protection of PII were instated, an important debate surrounding the following question emerged: *Would laws such as the European Union's General Data Protection Regulation (GDPR) impede technological advances or help address the challenge of data privacy?* Well, the answer to this question depends on several factors. I want to emphasize that while regulations are necessary, the proof of their effectiveness will rely on how they are implemented. Data privacy policies have to be proactive and evolve as the future of technology advances. Since the instatement of the GDPR, companies are struggling to adapt and comprehend that data privacy must be embedded in their business operation models.

The GDPR puts an emphasis on personally identifiable information (PII) which includes data such as your name, gender, ethnicity, phone number, email address, social security number, driver's license and social media profile. All of these attributes can be used to identify an individual. Therefore, organizations must ask and receive consent after providing a clear indication of how the data will be used prior to collection. This regulation has forced many companies to re-code their business models. A point of interest is the practice built on tracking the location, time spent online, websites visited, interests, and Internet protocol (IP) address of a customer in conjunction with PII. In the next chapter, I will discuss how to build systems that focus on data privacy by design as an integral part of your business model. It is also important to bring the notion of accountability to the forefront. There is no better time than now for conventions and rules that keep researchers, data analysts, data scientists, AI and machine learning engineers, companies, government agencies and everyone involved accountable as it pertains to collecting and handling personal data.

Why Does this Matter?

The General Data Protection Regulation (GDPR) which went into effect in May 2018, provides citizens with control over their personal data. It compels businesses to seek consent from their users while keeping them informed. This makes it easier to understand the choices available to them. It also establishes a strong enforcement mechanism of up to 4 percent of an enterprise's global revenue for non-compliance. The fine is broken down into 2 tiers (tier one is up to 2 percent for security breaches and tier two is 4 percent for individual privacy rights). In addition, the GDPR provides some relevant guidelines to addressing the growing risks of cyber-attacks while minimizing unethical use of personal sensitive data.

Non-compliance to the GDPR could impose significant costs on businesses. To draw an example of companies and potential penalties based on their 2017 global revenues, consider that some organizations with billions of dollars in revenue do not even make 4 percent in profits. The fine could exceed their profit margin or place them even further in the red. The only way out is to ensure that these corporations have a robust data protection and privacy policy in place. Highlighted below are a few companies and their potential fines based on their revenue in 2017.[136]

Company	HQ	Global Revenues ($M)	Profits ($M)	Non-compliance Penalties (fines will be applied to Global revenues)	
				Tier 1 (security breaches) 2%	Tier 2 (Individual privacy rights) 4%
Facebook	USA	$40,655	$15,934.0	$813.1	$1,626.2
Amazon	USA	$177,866	$3,033.0	$3,557.3	$7,114.6
Apple	USA	$229,234	$48,351.0	$4,584.7	9,169.4
Walmart	USA	$500,343	$9,662.0	$10,006.9	$20,013.7
Merck	USA	40,122	2,394.0	$802.4	$1,604.8
Target	USA	$71,879	$2,934.0	$1,437.6	$2,875.2
Verizon	USA	$126,034	$30,101.0	$2,520.7	$5,041.4
AT&T	USA	$160,546	$29,450.0	$3,210.9	$6,421.8
CVS Health	USA	$184,765	$6,622.0	$3,695.3	$7,390.6
Volkswagen	Germany	$260,028	$13,107.3	$5,200.6	$10,401.2
Daimler	Germany	$185,235	$11,863.9	$3,704.7	$7,409.4
Siemens	Germany	$91,585	$6,667.4	$1,831.7	$3,663.4
Toyota Motor	Japan	$265,172	$22,510.1	$5,303.4	$10,606.8
BP	UK	244,582	3,389.0	$4,891.6	$9,783.9

Prudential	UK	$111,458	$3,076.1	$2,229.2	$4,458.4
Samsung Electronics	South Korea	$211,940	$36,575.4	$4,238.8	$8,477.6
AXA	France	$149,461	$6,998.9	$2,989.2	$5,978.4
Total	France	$149,099	$8,631.0	$2,980.2	$5,960.4
Trafigura Group	Singapore	136,421	48,607.6	$2,728.4	$5,456.8
Sinopec Group	China	$326,953	$1,537.8	$6,539.1	$13,078.2
Huawei	China	$89,311	7,020.8	$1,786.2	$3,572.4
Alibaba	China	$37,771	$9,673.1	$755.4	$1,510.8
Tencent	China	$35,179	$10,580.6	$703.6	$1,407.2
Glencore	Switzerland	$205,476	$5,777.0	$4,109.5	$8,219.0

Sources: Fortune 500 (2018); Fortune Global 500 (2018)

Violating the GDPR privacy regulation could lead to a potential death sentence and force companies to delay their investments. Consider that some tech startups may need to constantly reinvest in order to grow their business. Some may have revenue, but are losing money—the GDPR would not take their situation into consideration. The company would still be fined up to 4 percent of their annual revenue. Walmart for example, has been the number 1 enterprise on the Fortune 500 list since 2013. While they had over $500 billion in revenue, they only made $9,862 billion in profits. A potential individual data privacy fine could cost the company more than $20 billion—which is more than double its profits.

California Consumer Privacy Act: Leading the Way

California leads the way with the most radical data protection and privacy regulation in the United States. The Golden State achieved a significant milestone by aiming to give consumers more control over their personal data with that policy. The passage of the Consumer Privacy Act in June 2018 landed on the heels of the EU's GDPR, which went into effect in May 2018. California's regulation could be vital in helping companies to prioritize the data privacy of their operations in the long run. This new law which is aimed at regulating how technology companies collect, store and process the data of their users, is set to go into effect in 2020. According to the *Wall Street Journal,* it has some similarities to the GDPR, but with distinctive applications. California's data privacy regulation protects consumers from data misuse and provides unprecedented protection for sensitive and personal data. This includes allowing them to opt out from having their personal data sold and requesting that it be deleted. The *Wall Street Journal* argues that the regulation "Imposed tough restrictions on the tech industry, potentially establishing a privacy template for the rest of the nation."[137]

10

A Road Map to Data Protection & Privacy

"We reject the excuse that getting the most out of technology means trading away your right to privacy... we choose a different path, collecting as little of your data as possible, being thoughtful and respectful when it's in our care because we know it belongs to you."[138]

—Tim Cook

There is no simple or magical blueprint to data privacy by design—it is a process that should become part of your organization's DNA and culture. To address this complex task, you must begin by making an assessment of your organization's data strategy and data privacy policy. I outline in this chapter a blueprint for data protection and privacy by design or by default following 7 key principles. The steps as defined are preliminary, yet vital as a baseline for your organization's business operation. Depending on the industry, they can be easily adapted if applied with discipline.

Back to the Basics

In chapter 7, I drew from examples of my previous work experience at a global research company in the greater Boston area. The lessons from the field, background and training bear enough relevance in my reflections on how I value data privacy—that is to adopt a risk-based approach. That said, let us go back to the basics. Part of my previous work involved collecting data on sensitive behavioral health from a very diverse group of subjects. We were required to follow rigorous practices that ranged from acquiring the Institutional Review Board (IRB) approval to developing strict guidelines that would protect the personal data of our subjects.

"All research that involves human subjects must be submitted to and approved by the IRB. The purpose of the IRB is to protect the rights of human subjects and to ensure the safety of all research participants."[139]

It was mandated that we inform our participants of the process and let them know how their data would be used. We also had to reassure them that their names and personal information would be masked and kept in the strictest of confidence. Finally, we could not proceed with data collection until we received their permission. To be precise, the consent was as valuable as the data we gathered. We began by using highly secured techniques to mask and encrypt all personal information. We also used ID codes and ensured that the stored personal identifiers were kept offline in secured servers; only authorized members of the research team were allowed to access the system. We would transfer and process data only by using identification codes. This was all back in early 2008—which is considered eons when the advancement of technology is concerned. The iPhone was just a year old and was only available in 4, 8 or 16 GB storage sizes. In 2018, a smartphone (Samsung Galaxy Note and iPhone Xs) goes up to 512GB in storage size. We have come such a long way and are progressing at an astronomical pace. Data has transformed every aspect of our lives and the efforts to protect it has all but gone by the wayside. To be sure it will be considered secondary until the risk becomes too great to ignore.

Protecting the confidentiality of the data for our study participants was designed as part of the research protocol. All instruments had to meet the IRB requirements—it became a means of privacy protection by default. Through the evolution of my career, this process has remained a key component of my work process. More specifically, the years spent collecting and analyzing highly sensitive data in behavioral health research helped me understand the critical importance of study protocol and data privacy.

With that in mind, a data analytics team must follow a number of general procedures which should guide how they adopt techniques that are aimed to protect and keep personal identification masked as much as possible. The confidentiality of subjects just a decade ago was largely considered a mandatory practice in many industries—particularly in human related studies. Our reputations and the successful outcome of our studies were predicated on protecting the privacy of our subjects. Any compromise would have been costly to the organization. What has changed since those years is the unchartered territory we find ourselves in—driven by automation as discussed in chapter 9.

Building Trust Has to Be Proactive

Enterprises must adopt a proactive rather than a reactive approach to data protection and privacy. The process should be mandatory if they are to consider the risks that data mismanagement could cost their operations. As previously indicated, re-coding your company's business model to include data protection and privacy will lead to significant gain as well as trust which is paramount for successful digital transformation.

Every application collects data from the moment a user hits download or install and at every click or swipe. As discussed in chapter 1, these applications know our best secrets and play a significant role in our daily lives. While some are built to be more aggressive in harvesting personal data, others are guilty of adopting creepy practices to track and collect our every move. Evidently, part of the solution to data privacy must come from within, simply put, at the source code. Technology companies that administer platforms and ecosystems to build and run applications such as Apple, Google, Facebook and Microsoft, can advance the process with necessary and strategic changes in their data privacy requirements for third party app developers to follow. This must be done to make the practice of developing apps more efficient, enhance privacy and ensure that the data of their users is protected. Again, Apple led the way; the company issued new guidelines in 2018 that aimed to compel developers to comply to strict data protection and privacy rules.

"Protecting user privacy is paramount in the Apple ecosystem, and you should use care when handling personal data to ensure you've complied with privacy best practices, applicable laws and the terms of the Apple Developer Program License Agreement, not to mention customer expectations."[140]

Do All Data Collection Methods Require Consent?

The answer to this is yes—by default. However, it depends upon several factors and raises a potential problem that is worth exploring and discussing. Let me begin by saying that the best practices for data protection and privacy which you will find covered in the next few pages must become your company's default option.

As a basic principle, any data that is being collected and may be subject to personally identifiable information (PII) must request consent from subjects beforehand—without any exceptions. Moreover, they must be informed about how and what their data will be used for. This process applies across the board—whether the data is being gathered on smart devices, online through the web, over email, applications, personal interviews, focus groups, or surveys. Additionally, as a guiding principle, when in doubt, it is always advisable to request permission.

According to the GDPR, *"Personal data is any information about an identified or identifiable person, also known as the data subject. Personal data includes information such as their: name, address, ID card/passport number, income, cultural profile, Internet Protocol (IP) address, data held by a hospital or doctor (which uniquely identifies a person for health purposes)."*[141]

In today's digital landscape where a simple viral hashtag can lead to the serious disruption of an enterprise, it is vital to ask for consent and store it as you value the data that you are collecting. Not only is this an ethical procedure, it is good for business. Storing your consent responses will be useful in assessing how you follow protocol and monitor the instances when the consent has been either misplaced or the data has not been properly collected or processed. Simply put, data protection and privacy must fit within your organization's way of doing business, and if well implemented will soon become second nature.

Data Protection and Privacy: Seven Key Principles–How Does Your Company Stack-up?

There is a wide interest in data privacy and its implication for businesses; however, the actual concrete practical guidance is lacking. My hope is that these basic principles will help managers, executives, data scientists, AI practitioners, and compliance specialists understand the risks and perform their functions while fully comprehending what is at stake in this very complex data-driven business landscape. Let us consider how companies that are collecting data could mitigate risks and adopt strict standards to protect, manage and monitor the data that belongs to their customers. It is important to understand that compliance measures are process-driven.

For starters, you can develop a plan to assess your company's current data gathering practices. Having a plan will absolutely reduce uncertainty and is an essential step in the process. This plan does not refer to simply adding disclaimers on your sites about cookies or sending emails with clauses in response to regulations. You will need to evaluate your data collection procedures though internal audits and a data protection impact assessment (DPIA)—this could be performed in specific cases and context. In the context of the GDPR, it applies to "A systematic and extensive evaluation of the personal aspects of an individual, including: profiling; processing sensitive data on a large scale; and systematic monitoring of public areas on a large scale."[142]

To be clear, a significant number of technology companies do not have data privacy standards in place. Some of these companies even built their business models by monetizing the personal data of their users, such as location-based tracking in real-time. Our daily lives are invaded with facial recognition technology (biometric software that has the ability to identify and authenticate faces of individuals from videos or digital images in real-time). Also considered to be powered by artificial intelligence, they (cameras) are constantly collecting our data without consent. Facial recognition systems are becoming predominant in our cities, stores, airports, police stations, our devices as well as in public, private and virtual spaces. When it comes to this technology, the genie is already out of the bottle. This is a sad reality. So, can it be fixed or even controlled? The stakes are high. Fixing it is absolutely imperative. The question to consider is what kind of policies would make sense if we are to consider the moving pace of technology? The focus should be on proactive privacy regulations that will guide its design as well as its deployment. This suggests containing its usage, particularly from being abused by both businesses and governments. The GDPR provides some guidelines, yet they are limited in scope regarding facial recognition technology (FRT) design and application. Focusing on regulations with effective oversight and accountability should be prioritized as if the future depends on policing and restricting its excessive usage—and it does. In addition to privacy, there is an inherent problem that is often reported which is imbedded bias. This could be considered as both: 1) the algorithm and 2) the process of selecting the training data used to train the system. Failing to fix the biases in facial recognition could cause irreparable harm to women and minorities—particularly black and young people. Additionally, it could be disruptive to businesses. As a result, various companies, including Microsoft, are urging governments worldwide to regulate facial recognition technology.

These companies gather data to help understand and serve their customers better, to create geo-behavior profiles and in some cases, to sell targeted services to business partners that are eager to know more about the interests and profiles of consumers. This type of data is generally compiled and stored without consent. In this new era, you must reevaluate third party partnerships and ensure you understand their existing business processes and privacy guidelines. The findings can be useful in addressing existing challenges as well as adopting proactive steps in developing a comprehensive protocol that will safeguard personally identifiable information (PII). As previously stated, the GDPR offers opportunities that go beyond EU members[143] to an extent, but data privacy will still need to become the core principle of all global trade initiatives, data flows and transactions. As a United Nations Conference on Trade and Development (UNCTAD) report on data protection and privacy describes, *"The current system of data protection is highly fragmented, with diverging global, regional and national regulatory approaches."*[144]

A Road Map

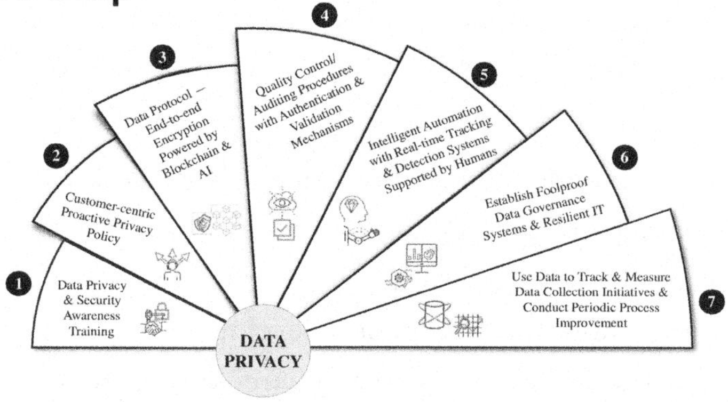

Seven Key Principles to Data Privacy by Design

1

Data protection and privacy must be an integral part of your enterprise's **data strategy.** Meaning, you must design the road map and place the privacy of your customers and employees at the heart of your organization's data procedures and ecosystem. This will pose as the core value system for the long-term health and effectiveness of your business. Next, you must define what privacy means for your company and how to gain and maintain the trust of your customers. The most important principle is that customers more than ever want to know how their data is being used—in a nutshell, they want to be in control of what rightfully belongs to them. Data privacy policies, such as the GDPR aim to change how organizations and government agencies are collecting and processing the data of their users/customers and citizens. A good start would entail providing all your employees with the right tools such as a basic **data privacy and security awareness training programs and activities** (practical and measurable simulations) to ensure that they understand the risk and are efficient and comfortable in their jobs. This will in turn add value to your business.

2

Adopt a customer-centric **Proactive Privacy Policy (PPP)** with clearly defined innovative and preventive measures aimed at ensuring the privacy, quality, integrity and reliability of data. This process will require that companies develop strategies to get closer to their customers or users beyond tracking their every move through technological means, thus overlooking the opportunity to build trust and potentially gain their loyalty. The real value of your data lies on its quality and the insights resulted from it. The shift in data privacy offers a company a unique opportunity to focus on quality and trust. When properly executed, this could lead to a more integrated and **symbiotic relationship** with customers. In return, these customers must be allowed to give and withdraw their consent and must be informed on how their data is being used. This will require establishing **customer-centered principles** as you train your employees on the high value of data protection and privacy. It is imperative that they understand the risk of compiling and processing data without consent as well as the indication of how the collected data will be used. Keep in mind that this strategy will require an all-inclusive approach with actionable and measurable steps—a complete culture shift.

3

As data, interconnected systems and processing powers continue to expand at an astronomical pace, organizations must define data protection, management and security protocols as an integral part of their business models. They need to identify clear guidelines for data collection, mining, storage, cleansing, processing and usage. Always adopt **End-to-end encryption** when gathering, storing and transferring data. Additionally, plan and implement procedures to anonymize data, particularly during a transfer. In short, create a method to mask sensitive and personally identifiable information (PII)—this could be costly to implement, but essential. Hardening your security protocol will lead to more secure platforms which can be reinforced with blockchain and artificial intelligence. Machine learning can be used to detect anomalies, finding patterns and conducting an in-depth network analysis to understand and uncover how potential threat actors could exploit weak links, breaches or vulnerabilities in your ecosystem. **Blockchain technology** tracks transactions, allows transparency in business processes and is tamper-proof. This technology has huge potential applications and use cases across various domains and industries particularly in storing and sharing data in a secured and trusted environment. However, as with any new technology, there are myriad of challenges and risks that have not yet been addressed, despite all the positive aspects. In the process, it is vital to adopt an integrated approach that would help safeguard your organization's digital ecosystem, thus minimizing risks and ensuring secure transactions. Building a proactive and predictive security ecosystem will aid in protecting the data of your customers. It is important to strike the right balance to ensure individual privacy as well as a more efficient use of data. This should never be a tradeoff.

4

Further, **Quality Control** procedures can be strengthened through a comprehensive evaluation of data collection practices and the continuous auditing of internal databases. Put some steps in place to assess the quality and integrity of data with **authentication** and **validation mechanisms**. Follow this up by responding and addressing any potential issues that could lead to data manipulation or breaches as quickly as possible. Quality control (QC) could be considered as an **auditing system** to ensure that the data collection methods follow protocol, are reliable, relevant and secure. This can be achieved by instituting an internal specified code of ethics with principles that range from compiling, storing, accessing, processing to analyzing data.

5

Your company's data infrastructure must follow data privacy by design as its core principle. This can be supported by the implementation of automated data protection tools to manage and store data in a secure blockchain system as previously indicated for example. An additional step would be to adopt **Intelligent Automation** with real-time tracking and detection systems that can identify trends, outliers and patterns in your organization's data. Intelligent automation powered by machine learning and artificial intelligence technology could be used to validate access to the ecosystem. Additionally, a routine report compiling each time the system is being accessed based on internal protocols, should be sent to the IT and data protection team. This process must include mechanisms that will verify the identification of all users which would in turn help prevent potential breaches. To ensure integrated protection, the intelligent automation infrastructure must be **supported by humans** to handle ambiguity and use judgment whenever necessary.

6

Understand that jeopardizing your public relations due to the potential outcry from customers could disrupt your business. When you fail to plan ahead to ensure that your organization follows data collection protocols, everything is placed at risk. As a result, you have to consider three key issues with the explosion of big data. 1) It is important and critical to put an emphasis on the quality of the data being collected. D**ata quality** is paramount for the success of your business. 2) Establishing foolproof **data governance** systems should serve as an operational model for your business and data management. 3) Determine which data is critical to your organization's survival and ensure that it is protected. This involves an all-inclusive and multi-pronged data security strategy to prevent technology related disruptions. It will require a particularly **resilient IT**, careful planning, and the best practices that must be followed and deeply-rooted in long-term efforts to build and support your company's ecosystem. Also required are data management best practices with protocols to manage and mitigate risk and the governance of the entire organization's data infrastructure.

7

Always use **Data** to track and measure your organization's data collection initiative—and to identify, detect and analyze trends, outliers and patterns in data processing and usage. This is essential to test how well your employees and automated systems comply to internal and external regulations as well as privacy protocols. Understanding how the data is compiled, handled, and processed will give your company a better shot at detecting potential compliance issues. This process will require you to consider gathering data on how internal policies are being followed. Data must be viewed as the most important asset of your enterprise thus, it should be used to assess progress throughout the ecosystems and apply insights to inform how you make decisions. It is also critical to put procedures in place that allow humans to conduct **periodic assessments** and monitor the performance of the system. **Documenting** the entire process will help you track and address any eventual threats to your data integrity as well as protecting your firm's reputation before potential issues become unmanageable. Use the insights generated from the analysis of your data privacy operations and go back to step 1—revise, adapt and improve your practices then move forward. While the process may appear to be tedious, it is a continuous loop towards operational excellence.

The effective implementation of these principles will depend largely on your organization's ability to identify the best possible solutions and collaborate with the right partners. It is important to understand that implementing new technologies requires broad collaboration, which could be a challenging burden in itself.

Data Privacy: A Business Imperative

There is no one-size-fits-all to data protection and privacy. You do not have to agree, validate, or adopt all of the specific steps. You must however, use some principles to guide your journey and act accordingly to ensure privacy and that the data of your customers or users and your enterprise's data are protected. This must be done by design as a vital component of your company's data strategy.

The solutions go beyond protecting your customer's data—it is imperative to your business. Your enterprise must develop meaningful strategies and insights to remain engaged with customers while building trust. To be clear, many companies are vulnerable to mishaps which vary from security breaches to product failure.

Government agencies and organizations of all professions must start exploring and testing various ways to build systems that will address this growing and disturbing concern before it becomes too big to handle. Not to be left out, government agencies, particularly, must redefine or readdress their processes and operations. As previously suggested, they should consider developing partnerships to ensure that ethical rules are established, and data is validated and classified accordingly. Data and analytics projects in addition to research studies should be valued and rated based upon the data sources that they employ and whether they follow data protection policies.

Managers in many corporations are often insulated from their customers depending on the size of the business. They manage though proxy and can become somewhat bureaucratic. It is important to recognize this potential trap and develop ways to facilitate quick and easy solutions for employees who are interacting directly with the data of your customers. The ability to communicate simply and respectfully with customers could help build trust and contain any potential conflicts that may arise.

The Increasing Risk of Contaminated Data

Threats come in varied forms and malicious acts to contaminate data are increasing at an alarming rate. Companies must avoid being caught between compiling massive amounts of data and cleaning up dubious content from their platforms. Leaving the data untreated could have serious repercussions on the bottom line and reputation of your business. They will also impact consumer and user confidence and contribute towards the decline of a company or brand's standing. Do not overlook the risk of crude, doctored images, conspiracies and content manipulation with evil motives that are easy to share and can spread quickly in the digital age and destroy reputations and lives. This has already caused serious and irreparable harm across the globe, far beyond the borders of the United States. This is a particularly worrisome issue in emerging and developing countries where social media platforms such as Facebook and YouTube have become the primary source of information for a significant majority of the population with internet access. These territories are highly vulnerable to all kinds of manipulations. To grasp the level of vulnerability in these countries, consider that the impact of these types of misinformation has already been encountered by some of the world's most advanced nations (the US, France and the UK). Fake content is an existential threat to our society and our democratic way of life.

A Pew Research Center Survey reported in 2017 that 67 percent of Americans indicated that "They got their news from social media."[145] The results also revealed that 66 percent were also Facebook users and almost half of Americans (45 percent) made Facebook their primary news source. Pew Research Center also reported that 18 percent of Americans today get their news from YouTube while 58 percent of them use it.[146] It is not terribly hard to understand the influence these big tech platforms hold or how their users are increasingly becoming targets for various stakeholders or interest groups from businesses, to government agencies, state-sponsored campaigns, politicians, and cyber threats.

Checks and Balances

A holistic strategy that cuts across all platforms is needed to tackle the contamination. Using machine learning and artificial intelligence technology to detect and contain defamatory data on social media platforms will play a significant role, *but not nearly enough*. I cover the complexity of this challenge in chapter 11. As a starting point, all automated data collection tools should bear warning signs to let users know how their data is being collected. This was the course of action previously observed when providing consent forms to respondents before conducting surveys, interviews or focus groups. With the risk being even greater in today's digital age, the checks and balances should be even more stringent. So, users can be cautioned and made aware of their interactions with an app or smart device with simple required warnings.

How the GDPR Changes the Data Privacy Paradigm

One of the most important parameters of the GDPR is that it follows European citizens wherever they interact with technology and however they transport their data as they travel the world. This principle-based regulation is broad, but purposely designed to have a wide impact on global data protection and privacy beyond the member states of the European Union. The regulation puts the power into the hands of the customer in order to control their data and places restrictions on centralized systems that have monetized and processed their data without consent. It is still unclear how this regulation will unfold, but it is safe enough to say that a wave of disruption is coming as customers become more aware and sensitive to their privacy protection. The storm is inevitable. The key principles of the GDPR have set the stage that could serve as guidelines for the global Internet Bill of Rights. This course of action will aid companies to mitigate the risks of data breaches that could disrupt them as we rapidly approach interconnected systems. Until then, enterprises regardless of location must manage to reconfigure their businesses to comply with the GDPR and make overall data protection an integral part of their business operation.

As we follow multiple cases of data misuse, social media platforms such as Facebook, Twitter, LinkedIn and Instagram have had to address privacy issues by restricting data access by third party apps and changing their APIs, short for application programming interface (tool used to interact, share, query or extract content and data from apps or websites). These restrictions have disrupted various companies whose business models were designed to process the data of social media users. Out of sheer desperation, some of these companies may choose to circumvent the restrictions which will lead to controversy. The controversy in return, would only be the tip of the iceberg that could lead to further demise. Those that seek ethical solutions will reinvent, and reengineer their business models while maintaining productive relationships with social media platforms, users and clients.

The Unknown

How much of the data that permeates our lives on a daily basis can be trusted? This is a question that cannot be answered with accuracy. What we do know is that data has been used in many different forms. It has been posed as a threat, as propaganda to influence our beliefs, and as a tool to save lives and improve our well-being. As we move toward interconnected systems, data privacy will continue to remain the pressing challenge of our time.

Additionally, as people, devices, robots, smart sensors, cameras, IoTs and all things around us interact to create highly integrated networks of connectivity powered by 5G technology, what steps will corporations and government agencies take to protect our privacy and gain our trust? By all indications, the risks for data privacy and security will continue to grow exponentially. It is important to understand the type of connectivity that will be permitted and how the processing of data will have a direct impact on our lives. If a well thought out solution is not conceived, the advancement of technology will be in jeopardy. I hope appropriate regulations will be conceived not to impede, but to encourage innovation. By working towards a solution collectively, the future of interconnected systems will be nothing short of exciting. Until then, we are confined to whirling in a world of great uncertainty.

PART FIVE

BETTER TOGETHER: HUMANS + MACHINES

11

Where Do We Go from Here?

"Better Together. Understanding this key attribute and finding the equilibrium between humans + machines remains a serious equation that smart enterprises need to resolve in order to stay viable in business."

—Journel Joseph

Be Ready for What Is Next: The Conundrum of Data Privacy and Trust in the Digital Age

Trust is the glue that binds a company and its consumers together in the digital age. Any form of embedded bias could disrupt that trust. And it is important to emphasize that a public crisis associated with any level of prejudice that has been encoded in a company's AI-powered ecosystem could lead to a revolt from their customers. Ultimately, the cost of fixing that problem could be as significant as a total disruption in a volatile business landscape. It is in the best interest of an organization to ensure that data and algorithms are passed through a gauntlet to sustain their quality and validity. This will require a framework to ensure that appropriate governance and accountability mechanisms are put into place for data quality and reliability. It is also important to be cautious in the understanding that not all data and algorithms are "created equal." There are legitimate business reasons for prioritizing diversity in the selection of teams as well as training data. This will serve as a driving force to building the future and staying ahead of your competitors.

The Reckoning

Artificial Intelligence at its core, is a byproduct of data and algorithms which comes with some serious and potential ethical risks. As Greg Brockman defines it, "AI systems are built on three foundations: algorithms, data, and computing (or amounts of computational resources)."[147] Can an AI be trained to discriminate? Based on the data it is fed—this is very possible, and can lead to severe challenges within our society. In a simple and very basic approach, it helps to consider AI as an athlete in training to run a marathon. Its diet, nutrition, eating habits and countless hours of practice will be reflected in its performance on the trail. Then, to ensure success, it requires an action plan with a clear vision, strategy, persistence, determination, grit, and a particularly great team and support system. The ability to measure progress along the way with the understanding that success is built off continuous improvement, is essential. It is a journey through which small wins will keep it motivated and stayed on course. As you move forward, it is fundamental to be constantly reminded that building models and algorithms or feeding AI data that contains prejudice or any kind of bias, will simply produce biased systems, which in turn, will deliver bad insights and cause serious harm to a business and to humanity as a whole.

Implementing AI in your business process is vital for your organization. It is important to understand that it can bring both benefits and risks as previously mentioned, and such an endeavor requires a deep dive into the core values of your enterprise. Corporate executives and government officials must understand that behavior such as (prejudice) could leave them vulnerable. Data scientists, engineers and data and analytics professionals, must be cautious and ensure that their algorithms do not lead to unintended consequences. If the primary goal is to improve productivity and augment human ability (getting it right), organizations must ensure that the model reflects the general resemblance of the people it has been designed for. Companies must also develop ethical guidelines and ask the right questions as they are integrating AI into their business practices and moving towards the future. The very fact that such risks are looming over the future is puzzling. It is critical that your business is prepared for a moment of reckoning. There are good reasons to question whether AI will adopt a path that is similar to the apps and whether its usage will distribute across the world. *Will it manifest in the form of complete domination and impose itself to those in developing and emerging countries or the marginalized in developed countries? Will they be equipped with the power to engage and enforce regulations?* It is uncertain exactly how this will unfold. As I envision the future, I can only hope that the leading corporations will uphold the world to a better standard as demonstrated through the launch of the Apple App Store and Google Play which are accessible to (almost) everyone. Obviously, data privacy remains a serious puzzle in the age of apps.

Across the Globe: Data Protection & Privacy Policies

"It is important to consider that context can turn non-sensitive data into sensitive data. The context in which the data is used (e.g. cultural, geographic, religious, political circumstances, etc.) may influence the effect of the data analysis of an individual or group of individuals, even if that data is not explicitly personal or sensitive."[148] United Nations Development Group (UNDP).

This is crucial as cross-border data flows are growing increasingly at a rapid pace. As a 2016 McKinsey report puts it "While the trade of global goods and financial flows have flattened since the Great Recession, cross-border flows of data are surging. Today's digital form of globalization is changing who is participating, how business is being done across borders, how rapidly the competition moves, and where the economic benefits are flowing."[149]

According to the results of a 2018 United Nations data privacy study, "107 countries (of which 66 were developing or transition economies), have put legislation in place to secure the protection of data and privacy."[150] The UN's assessment indicated that 57 percent of countries worldwide have legislation, 10 percent have already drafted regulation, 21 percent have no laws regarding data protection and privacy, and data was completely unavailable for 12 percent. The UN's tracking system also revealed that from "138 countries (of which 95 are developing and transition economies), had enacted cybercrime legislation."[151] Over 30 percent of these countries did not have any laws in place against cybercrime. I want to underline that the concerns about individual privacy rights and their data are well-grounded and necessary however, it is important to conceive and design policies in the process that will not impede data flows or create barriers that risk leading to what is described as "digital protectionism."

The Quest to Data Privacy: The Least Developed Countries Are Left Behind

Data protection and privacy has become an absolute global concern. In addition to implementing data protection and privacy principles to protect their citizens, the biggest challenge for developing nations would be the high cost and resources to enforce and fine the violators. This course of action can be costly without the right expertise and the proper mechanisms in place (such as conducting investigations on potential violators of data protection and privacy). According to the United Nations Conference on Trade and Development (UNCTAD)[152] less than 40 countries in Asia and Africa were reported to have a regulation in place. Additionally, only 16 (34 percent) of 47 less developed countries have established a data protection and privacy legislation. This is in stark comparison to 98 percent of the countries in Europe (including non-European Union members) that have currently enacted policies. As we begin to discover, the GDPR's authority and capability to investigate and punish violators is prompting companies to develop systems that ensure compliance. This is a direct result of the European Union's power to enforce regulations and a mandate that fines companies that fail to comply with data privacy up to 4 percent of the company's worldwide annual revenue.

"No one shall be subjected to arbitrary interference with his privacy…"[153] Universal Declaration of Human Rights.

What Is Up with Our Data: A Cautionary Tale

Organizations have unlimited access to our data and consequently, our lives. They certainly use the data to offer us targeted ads, improved the user experience (UX) and finding cures for diseases. They also aim to design new products, understand the behavior of customers, and help moderate activities on their platforms. The data attracts various types of attacks—including, malware and spam, phishing (deceptive websites designed to mislead users into believing they are real, then revealing for example, their credit card or sensitive information). The irony is that the privacy we are seeking cannot exist without the use of data. To be clear, this encapsulates the dilemma that both users and companies find themselves in. We can call it the user conundrum—the perfect juxtaposition of the good and the bad. That said, privacy should not be a tradeoff, and data protection and privacy must be available to all— "it is a basic human right." As I discussed in chapter 10, it is also a business imperative and companies must develop mechanisms to enforce internal compliance. This includes compiling data as discussed in the 7 principles, to evaluating data gathering by employees and cognitive systems. Companies are absolutely obligated to inform users or customers about how they are collecting and using their data.

Data is as important to a business operation's efficiency as water is to a human's thirst and body function. If you do not possess it, you must acquire it. If it becomes contaminated, it must be treated before further use. Failing to do so could cause a grave illness or even death. With that considered, it is safe to say that making data-driven decisions is a matter of survival for every business.

The Facebook Conundrum

In May 2018, I streamed the video of the founder and CEO of Facebook, Mark Zuckerberg's keynote address at the company's F8 Developers Conference. He covered varied subjects including the future of artificial intelligence and virtual reality (VR). Following events from previous months about data privacy, I was curious to hear about the forthcoming potential changes. I watched a few more videos on the Facebook for Developers website to grasp a broader picture of the company's vision for the future. It was then that I began to consider the enormity of challenge related to its massive number of users. The numbers are so astronomical that I had to look beyond them. I will discuss some of the challenge in the next section but for now, let us first dwell on the complexity of managing and moderating the activities of over 1.47 billion active *daily* users. In comparison, this has surpassed the population of China (1.41 billion people according to United Nations DESA[154] projections), and Facebook has since reported more than 2.23 billion monthly active users as of June 2018.[155] Users are located across varied geographic locations and communities, and possess a diversity of cultural, political and religious beliefs as well as a complexity of languages spoken. Consider the vast complexity of "hundreds" of languages interacting and generating endless amounts of content by the second. Literally, billions of texts, voice messages, videos, and images are being generated on the Facebook platform and its various apps every single day. Mark Zuckerberg also revealed during the F8 Developers Conference that there were over 2 billion minutes of private voice notes and video calls on WhatsApp, in addition to over 65 billion messages shared daily on the app in 2017.[156] Keep in mind that for most social media networks, privacy did not really matter or become a priority until it became too complex to handle. They are still ill-prepared to address the enormity and complexity of the challenge related to data misuse and manipulation.

When the World Goes Social: Behind the Numbers

Threat actors are a legitimate concern and have invaded the same systems that we use to transmit our thoughts and interactions with our family, friends and loved ones. They implant contaminated content and dubious data through the very same languages that we communicate in. To get a sense of the enormity of this challenge, consider that according to the U.S. Census Bureau,there are over 350 languages spoken in homes across the U.S. alone.[157] Further, the Ethnologue estimates that there are over 7,000 world languages.[158] While not all of these languages are being used on social network platforms, a significant number of them are. The vast cultural diversity and differences in languages and usage can be challenging to monitor and manage if we are to consider the context, nuances and emotional aspects of these conversations even with the most advanced technology. These languages vary significantly in how they are constructed. What we know, assume, and how we analyze data is often influenced by our limited perception of the world. At this early stage, AI can only efficiently execute what it is trained to do, based on the data that it is fed. Moderating such complex systems with content that is constantly being inundated by the second in hundreds of languages is truly a conundrum. Each language or even dialect has a unique syntax (structure and order), semantics (meaning), phonology and phonetic features (pronunciation), and lexicon (vocabulary). As a polyglot, I am constantly learning and exploring different languages and I completely understand the complexity and challenge entailed when interpreting context—particularly digital texts. They can be very difficult to translate from one language to another. Context can often lead to ambiguity. One word that is used in a specific context in one language may be perceived as offensive in another. Another basic example would be the use of gender in romance languages. "The car" translated in 3 different languages (French, German, Spanish) have different structures. The gender is feminine in French (La voiture), neutral in German (Das Auto), and masculine in Spanish (El coche).

Social Networking in an Uncertain Time

The consortium of social network platforms serves more than simply facilitating communication and networking, they have also become social phenomena that are deeply intertwined in our culture. Unless all data misuses and breaches are consistently ignored and become a recurring issue that repeatedly causes harm—Facebook, YouTube, WhatsApp, Twitter, Instagram, Snapchat and other social media platforms will remain a valuable and cultural force in our society. A customer's revolt however, should never be overlooked. Data has redefined the global business landscape and the rules of the game have yet to be written. The main question is, *How are companies going to face the future in this tumultuous and uncertain time?*

Be Aware. Humans Are Underrated.

The fear about the future of companies and their staff is centered around the unknown role that artificial intelligence will play in society. We have settled on the reality that smart automation will improve our lives and augment the productivity of the workforce. What has always remained uncertain is the right proportion and balance of human-machine to build an efficient workforce. We started to detect a slow trend that revealed that overusing robots in a company's production line could lead to inverse impact such as stagnation and reduced performance. This real-world experience began to become apparent in the following example from Tesla. Tesla is considered to be the pioneer of electric vehicles (EVs) and the leading manufacturer of smart automobiles that have one of the world's most advanced robotics and automated production factory. As the *New Times* reported, the company's prediction to "Produce 20,000 Model 3s a month by December 2017,"[159] did not pan out as planned. It is reported that they only manufactured 2,425 of the Model 3s during the final three months of that year. Evidently, the high-speed, high-tech and sophisticated AI-powered assembly line did not work as planned. As robots faulted out or crashed, they slowed down the production process and created bottlenecks, admitted Elon Musk, the CEO of Tesla. In order to rectify the problem, they had to bring the humans to do what they do best thus, embracing the symbiotic humans-machines relationship. Despite the exciting advancement of AI in the manufacturing process, the fully automated system is still a risky bet.

Elon Musk also admitted during an interview on CBS in April 2018, with Gayle King,[160] that his company's excessive reliance on automation to build the mass-market Model 3 vehicles may have impeded its production. He responded to the critics who argued that too many sophisticated robots could have been part of the cause of the production nightmare that the company faced when attempting to meet its demand. Elon Musk agreed. In response to Tim Higgins, a *Wall Street Journal* (WSJ) technology and auto reporter's tweet on April 13, 2018, on the issue, he responded, *"Yes, excessive automation at Tesla was a mistake. To be precise, my mistake. Humans are underrated."*[161] Various companies will also eventually discover this hard truth and it might come at a steep price due to over automation. Regrettably, it could also lead to an irreparable disarray in the ecosystems of many companies.

The Path Forward: Humans + Machines Working Together

Hopefully, smart organizations and leaders will learn from Tesla's lessons and adjust their plans accordingly. Companies need to reinvent their workforce while they are building smart systems. In June 2018, it was reported that the company produced 5,000 Model 3 vehicles per week to finally reached its long-delayed goal. With a more symbiotic workforce (humans + machines), Tesla slightly exceeded its mass-market Model 3 production target with over 55,000 vehicles in the third quarter of 2018 and the company will eventually reach the next frontier—achieving profitability. It is imperative that they do not underestimate the value and capabilities of humans in the process. Understanding this key attribute and finding the equilibrium between humans-machines remains a serious equation that smart enterprises need to resolve in order to stay viable in business. A hybrid model, for example, is a likely scenario that should be seriously considered. Deloitte describes this as a "Symbiotic relationship of the human-machine workforce."[162] If you are designing and thinking about adopting AI-powered automated systems that will take over the world and replace rather than enhance humans, it might be time to forsake that train of thought. As we are still in the early days in AI development, we can learn from the wide adoption and successes of the apps in our smart devices—they have changed everything to the point where we entrust them with our secrets and most cherished memories. Further, they even help us navigate unfamiliar territories. The secret is simple—designing products and services that are open to all and not selective to specific demographics, geographic locations, or prices will enrich the lives of its users.

Better Together

Contrary to the past when various companies failed due to the delay in adopting technology, the future's disruption might come from underrating humans, overusing robots and failing to build a symbiotic workforce for the future. As we embark on the quest to advance toward smart automation, it is imperative to find the interwoven path to building systems that are operable and accessible to all, thereby enabling people and machines to work together. The understanding that humans make and should ultimately operate machines, brings us closer to a perfect balance for a collective, efficient and unstoppable workforce—a workforce that will dominate the world without hidden fears of the unknown. Is it tangible? Absolutely—as long as we work fearlessly, intelligently and collectively. As the saying goes, *united* we will absolutely thrive, but *divided*, well—our fall will be nothing short of inevitable.

Acknowledgments

No form of writing can be accomplished in isolation. The influence, assistance and inspiration of others is invaluable and represents the soul of the work. To that end, I must acknowledge all of my friends, colleagues, loved-ones, sponsors, advisors and mentors who have worked tirelessly in various ways to inspire and support me through this journey over the years. This book in actuality, is as much their achievement as it is mine.

As I reflect back on my career and training, I owe a huge debt of gratitude to professor Anna Madison. I have learned vastly from her. I doubt that I would have embarked on this rewarding career of data and analytics had our paths not crossed. Her influence in shaping my career and enriching my thinking over the years goes well beyond what I could express in just a few lines.

I am also indebted to Joan Parker, who graciously served as my writing coach for 5 years (2003-2008).

Authors are often credited for their work; I can personally attest to that, but I am positive that all great writers would admit that their work would not be as successful without an amazing editor. I have been fortunate to have met and worked with Lilian

N. Blankson, whose dedication, experience and intellect made this book much better than it would have otherwise been. I often refer to her as a blessing—indeed, she is. As a gifted editor, she poured her heart into editing the manuscript and spent countless hours, often deep into the night improving its fluidity through various iterations. I would receive occasional text messages at three in the morning asking me to upload the next chapter, so she could work on it in the morning. Lilian does everything with passion and her commitment to this book goes beyond what words can ever describe.

I am profusely grateful to Michael Dutton for the countless hours spent proofreading the manuscript despite his hectic schedule. Michael is an amazing editor and corporate communications strategist—his insightful suggestions, recommendations and comments on numerous chapters largely contributed to help make this book a useful tool for readers. I am convinced this project would not have come to fruition without his editing on the first draft—encouragement and assistance over the years.

I am thankful for all the help received from Lenz Bayas, Jacob Dornevil and Nicolas Andre in preparing and reviewing the manuscript from the early days to its completion. They provided me with insightful and critical feedback, and helpful guidance. They saw the potential in my vision and continuously supported and encouraged me to pursue and create the work.

I want to especially thank Miguel Marling, whose hours of conversation, intelligent critique and ideas helped shape the concept and framework for the manuscript.

I wish to acknowledge Ghislain Viau for his professionalism, talent and extent of his work from the cover design, the interior layout and overall formatting of the book.

I am particularly grateful to have worked with Leslie Goodyear, President of the American Evaluation Association (AEA). As my supervisor during the early stages of my career, she afforded me unique opportunities to learn and grow, which in turn significantly reinforced my interest in technology, research, evaluation, data and analytics. I also wish to acknowledge some great colleagues from the various organizations I have worked for over the years: Calynn Evans, Lisa Welch, Beth Mason, Deborah McCall, Damon Williams, Verna Robinson, Michael Dutton, Emily Elstad, Lorna Walters and Dwight Fee.

I was privileged as a graduate student from the Fletcher School of Law and Diplomacy and the Department of Urban & Environmental Policy and Planning (UEP), Graduate School of Arts and Sciences at Tufts University, to work with and learn from some world-renowned scholars and dynamic practitioners who have molded my thinking and inspired me. I would especially like to thank my advisors Carsten Kowalczyk, Francine Jacobs and James Jennings—they taught me to always look and think outside the box for solutions to complex issues. I want to particularly thank Deborah Winslow Nutter, Senior Associate Dean and Director of the Global Master of Arts Program (GMAP) at the Fletcher School, for inspiring and motivating me and many others around the world to develop a 360-degree perspective of the complex global landscape to succeed and to make a difference. I wish to also acknowledge the following Professors: Robert Burdick, Joel P. Trachtman, Richard Shultz, Robert Pfaltzgraff, Bernard Simonin, Lawrence Krohn, Laurent Jacques, Julian Agyeman, Ingar Palmlund, Erin Seaton, Penn Loh, Laurie Goldman, Barbara Parmenter, and especially Mary Davis, Chair of the Department of Urban &

Environmental Policy and Planning (UEP). I am also grateful to my former professors at the University of Massachusetts, College of Public and Community Service (CPCS): Anna Madison, Joan Arches, Elaine Ward, Ann Whitorn, Fred Johnson and Cuf Ferguson.

I am deeply grateful to Professor James Calvin of John Hopkins University for his extraordinary wisdom and valuable insight and perspective during our many conversations about technology, interconnected systems, IoTs, as well as the impact of artificial intelligence (AI) and digitalization on the future of the global workforce.

I wish to acknowledge D. Keith Pigues—a simple conversation between us sparked so much insight and helped me approach this book with a renewed focus for my readers on adapting the key issues that pertain to the real world, as well as incorporating memorable examples and key takeaways.

I would like to highlight the constant inspiration from the GMAP 13, a network of global leaders from the Fletcher School with whom I have learned to expand my boundaries and accomplish things that will impact the world; no matter how miniscule those things may appear to be.

Mom and Dad, I thank you so much for the discipline, hard work, perseverance, courage, the love for learning and the powerful belief in humanity that goes beyond self-worth that you instilled in me. You have taught me that it does not matter how far or where I came from in life—what matters most is how to make a difference in the lives of others. You have also enabled me to understand that regardless of how successful I am—what is most paramount is the manner in which I treat, value and respect others. I would not be where I am without your priceless lessons, prayers, guidance and assistance. Had it not been for your support, I would have given up many times in the past when things did not work in my favor. Your unconditional support, love and constant prayers are the sole reason why I have made it this far.

A special person was involved in this journey and to her, I am most thankful. A heartfelt thank you goes to Valerie Laplante for her unyielding support and belief in me. Her encouragement and motivation played an essential part in the completion of this book. I also want to relay particular appreciation to her mother, Mildred Ebanks, for her motivation and encouragement throughout this process.

I am truly grateful to my family and loved-ones for their unconditional love and support of me over the years: Jean Fenel Detant, Guerda Victorin, Edith & Gerald Boulin, Michaelle Felix, Fritzner Detant, Esther Celestin Wang and Ruth Roberson. To my amazing sister Naomie Joseph Dornevil and brother Wickenson Joseph, for their ongoing support and inspiration. You guys brought significant and unfaltering grace and blessings to my life. Nao and Jacob, thank you for your unwavering support of all my endeavors over the years; regardless of whether they resulted in success or failure. I could not have done it without you.

I want to especially thank Antoine Junior Melay for his genuine support, and the conversations we had about strategies and entrepreneurship have influenced my approach. I wish to acknowledge Gireaud Joseph, Miller Germain, Morisset Saint Preux, Richard Raymond, Juliano Noel, Jean Fenel Detant, and Lamos Paul for their cheerful support in many ways over the years and throughout the long journey of writing this book.

I am very grateful to all the friends who shared ideas, supported, believed and encouraged me over the years. I have learned greatly from Rachel Bayas, Maxiana Noel, Kenisha Salvatory, James Antoine, Carline Morney, Yveline Alteon, Benjamin Jerome, Ruthza Olivier Rimpel, Debbie Rateau, Ulysse Johnson, Ernst Andre, Bernard Julien, Mildred Jean, Serge Chery, Morisset Saint Preux, Louise Raymond, Ronald Paul, Alfred P. Noel, Richard and Naomie Nicolas, Nona Raphael and Jobnel Pierre.

I would also like to acknowledge the following friends I have met over the past few years who have challenged, inspired and motivated my passion for this incredible field and making a difference in the world: Emily Artiano, Amna-Noor Al-Gallas, Aziza Mohamed, Joseph Rostand Biwole, Alexandra Pribilovics, Amb. Guillian Bristol, Robert Avetisyan, James Bauler, Irene Mbari-Kirika & Kirika Mugo, Irasema Infante & Amb. Geronimo Gutiérrez, Bernard Zongo, Luis Viguria, Kristina Yates, Robinson Cook & Paula Fynboh, Monica Smith, Melanie Reed, Adrian Lagrama, Alexis Vanderhye and John Smith.

I owe an enormous debt of gratitude to the pioneers in the field of AI, Big Data, Research, Evaluation, Management and Strategy. They have worked tirelessly in the dark over the years and their persistence and ingenuity has incredibly enlightened and transformed the everyday lives of people worldwide. Some are no longer alive to see the AI rush, but their contribution lives on. I am grateful to have been exposed to the work of world-renowned AI and Machine Learning experts such as Manuela Veloso of Carnegie Mellon University, JT Kostman of Grant Thornton, Fei-Fei Li of Sandford University, Thomas Malone and Max Tegmaf of MIT, Geoffrey Hinton of the University of Toronto, and AI pioneers, John McCarthy, Alan Turing, Norbert Weiner—research gurus Michael Q. Paton, Robert Stake, Thomas H. Davenport, Bernard

H. Russell, management gurus Peter Drucker, Russell L. Ackoff, and Professors William Moomaw and Bhaskar Chakravorti of Tufts University. Their writing and work collectively, have inspired, influenced and molded my thoughts far beyond the few citations that appear in this book.

I am also grateful to the researchers, engineers and data scientists that make the field of data and analytics so exciting and intriguing. Further, I am indebted to some of the world's most renowned organizations and publications that are quoted in this book. Their insight has inspired me significantly.

Finally, I would like to thank the Smithsonian group of museums not only for serving as a safe refuge for me over the years, but for enabling us all to be exposed to the evolution of humanity and the history of innovation. They built the foundation that fostered the belief of a better future for the world at large deep within me.

And most importantly, I want to humbly thank God Almighty for guiding and bestowing me with the inspiration, intellect, vision, wisdom, and foresight to write this book.

NOTES

1 General Data Protection Regulation (GDPR, 2016). Regulation (EU) 2016/679 of the European Parliament and of the Council. Official Journal of the European Union. Retrieved from https://eur-lex.europa.eu/legal-content/EN/TXT/PDF/?uri=CELEX:32016R0679. https://gdpr-info.eu

2 Abbatiello, A., Boehm, T., Schwartz, J., Chand, S. (2017). No-collar Workforce: Humans and Machines in One Loop—Collaborating in Roles and New Talent Models. Tech Trends 2018: The Symbiotic Enterprise. Deloitte University Press.

3 Apple (2008). Apple Introduces the New iPhone 3G: Twice as Fast at Half the Price. Apple Press Release. Retrieved from https://www.apple.com/newsroom/2008/06/09Apple-Introduces-the-New-iPhone-3G/

4 Apple (2008). Apple Sells One Million iPhone 3Gs in First Weekend. Apple Press Release. Retrieved from https://www.apple.com/newsroom/2008/07/14Apple-Sells-One-Million-iPhone-3Gs-in-First-Weekend/

5 App Annie (2018). 2017 Retrospective: A Monumental Year for the App Economy. Retrieved from https://www.appannie.com/en/insights/market-data/app-annie-2017-retrospective/

6 NASA: From Hidden to Modern Figures: NASA's Past Shows the Way to the Future. Retrieved from https://www.nasa.gov/modernfigures/

7 NASA: From Hidden to Modern Figures. Katherine Johnson Biography. Retrieved from https://www.nasa.gov/content/katherine-johnson-biography

8 National Geographic (2011). Flying Under the Radar: A History of Stealth Planes. Retrieved from https://www.nationalgeographic.com.au/engineering/flying-under-the-radar-a-history-of-stealth-planes.aspx

9 Long T. (2008, February 2). Feb. 26, 1935: Radar, The Invention that Saved Britain. Wired. Retrieved from https://www.wired.com/2008/02/dayintech-0226/

10 Kurt W. Beyer (2009). Grace Hopper and the Invention of the Information Age. MIT Press

11 The Smithsonian: The National Museum of American History Museum. Exhibition Hall

12 NASA. Your Device Has More Computing Power. Retrieved from https://www.nasa.gov/mission_pages/voyager/multimedia/vgrmemory.html#.W5wXfehKiUk

13 IBM (2013). 2.5 Quintillion Bytes of Data Created Every Day. How Does CPG & Retail Manage It? https://www.ibm.com/blogs/insights-on-business/consumer-products/2-5-quintillion-bytes-of-data-created-every-day-how-does-cpg-retail-manage-it/

14 Facebook (2018). F8 Developer Conference. Retrieved from https://developers.facebook.com/videos

15 Morris, C. (2017, January 9). 8 Ways Steve Jobs Changed the Cellphone World 10 Years Before the iPhone X. CNBC. Retrieved from https://www.cnbc.com/2017/09/15/8-ways-steve-jobs-changed-the-telecommunications-industry.html

16 Apple (2008). Apple Sells One Million iPhone 3Gs in First Weekend. Apple Press Release. Retrieved from https://www.apple.com/newsroom/2008/07/14Apple-Sells-One-Million-iPhone-3Gs-in-First-Weekend/

17 Steve Jobs (2008): Apple WWDC 2008—iPhone 3G Introduction.

18 Resnick, M. (2016). Defining Mobile Solutions in a Post-App Era. Gartner. Retrieved from https://www.gartner.com/doc/3540034/defining-mobile-solutions-postapp-era

19 McKinley, J. (2009). MapQuest: A Symbol of Everything That's Gone Wrong. Business Insider. Retrieved from https://www.businessinsider.com/mapquest-a-symbol-of-everything-thats-gone-wrong-2009-2

20 Smithsonian Magazine (2012). How Steve Jobs' Love of Simplicity Fueled a Design Revolution. Retrieved from https://www.smithsonianmag.com/arts-culture/how-steve-jobs-love-of-simplicity-fueled-a-design-revolution-23868877/

21 Gartner (2014). Newsroom: Gartner Reveals 2014 Mobility Predictions. Retrieved from https://www.gartner.com/newsroom/id/2648515

22 App Annie (2018). 2017 Retrospective: A Monumental Year for the App Economy. Retrieved from https://www.appannie.com/en/insights/market-data/app-annie-2017-retrospective/

23 Smithsonian Magazine (2012). How Steve Jobs' Love of Simplicity Fueled a Design Revolution. Retrieved from https://www.smithsonianmag.com/arts-culture/how-steve-jobs-love-of-simplicity-fueled-a-design-revolution-23868877/

24 Bloomberg Technology (2018). Bloomberg Technology: Addressing the Anxiety Over AI. Emily Chang Interview with Greg Brockman on June 26, 2018. Bloomberg. Retrieved from https://www.bloomberg.com/news/videos/2018-06-27/addressing-the-anxiety-over-ai-video

25 U.S. Congress (2018). Testimony of Mr. Greg Brockman, Co-founder of Open AI, a Non-profit Artificial Intelligence Development Organization. Retrieved from https://docs.house.gov/meetings/SY/SY15/20180626/108474/HHRG-115-SY15-Wstate-BrockmanG-20180626.pdf

26 Bloomberg Technology (2018). Bloomberg Technology: Addressing the Anxiety Over AI. Emily Chang Interview with Greg Brockman on June 26, 2018. Bloomberg. Retrieved from https://www.bloomberg.com/news/videos/2018-06-27/addressing-the-anxiety-over-ai-video

27 Rao, A. S. (2014). Social Listening: How Market Sensing Trumps Market Research. PwC. Resilience: A Journal of Strategy and Risk.

https://www.pwc.com/gx/en/governance-risk-compliance-consulting-services/resilience/publications/pdfs/social-listening.pdf

28 Nielsen (2016): A New Megaphone: Social Media Gives Consumers a Chance to be Heard on What They Watch. Retrieved from https://www.nielsen.com/us/en/insights/news/2017/a-new-megaphone-social-media-gives-consumers-a-chance-to-be-heard.html

29 Jacobson, I; Spence, I. & Bittner, K. (2011). Use Case 2.0: The Guide to Succeeding with Use Cases. Ivar Jacobson International

30 Poetz, M., Franke, N., & Schreier M. (2014): Sometimes the Best Ideas Come from Outside Your Industry. Harvard Business Review (HBR). Retrieved from https://hbr.org/2014/11/sometimes-the-best-ideas-come-from-outside-your-industry

31 Benson-Armer, R., Noble, S., & Thiel, A. (2105). The Consumer Sector in 2030: Trends and Questions to Consider. McKinsey: Consumer Packaged Goods Practice. https://www.mckinsey.com/industries/consumer-packaged-goods/our-insights/the-consumer-sector-in-2030-trends-and-questions-to-consider

32 Hawkins, D. M. (1980). Identification of Outliers. Chapman and Hall. London – New York

33 Repenning, N. P., Kieffer, D., & Astor, T. (2017): The Most Underrated Skill in Management. MIT Sloan Review. Retrieved from http://sloanreview.mit.edu/article/the-most-underrated-skill-in-management/

34 Andriotis, A. (2017, October 18). American Express CEO to Step Down After 16 Years. The Wall Street Journal (WSJ). Retrieved from https://www.wsj.com/articles/american-express-ceo-kenneth-chenault-to-step-down-1508358151

35 Shaban, H. (2017, June 13). It's official: Verizon finally buys Yahoo. Washington Post. Retrieved from https://www.washingtonpost.com/news/the-switch/wp/2017/06/13/its-official-verizon-finally-buys-yahoo/?noredirect=on&utm_term=.b5430d6245a7

36 Goel, V. & J. de la Merced, M. (2016, July 24). Yahoo's Sale to Verizon Ends an Era for a Web Pioneer. New York Times. Retrieved from https://www.nytimes.com/2016/07/25/business/yahoo-sale.html

37 Nicas, J. (2016, July 25). What is Yahoo? Riddle Plagued CEOs for Two Decades. Wall Street Journal (WSJ). Retrieved from https://www.wsj.com/articles/what-is-yahoo-riddle-plagued- ceos-for-two-decades-1469446207

38 Google Cloud Platform (2016). What's Next for Big Data. Retrieved from https://cloud.google.com/products/big-data/

39 Pullen, J. P. (2017, April 24). Google's Parent Company Achieves Big Market Cap Milestone. Fortune. Retrieved from http://fortune.com/2017/04/24/alphabet-google-market-cap-valuation/

40 Ferris, R. (2017, April 10). Tesla Passes General Motors to Become the Most Valuable U.S. Automaker. CNBC. Retrieved from https://www.cnbc.com/2017/04/10/tesla-passes-general-motors-to-become-the-most-valuable-us-automaker.html

Welch, D. (2017, April 10). Tesla Just Passed GM to Become America's Most Valuable Carmaker. Bloomberg. Retrieved from https://www.bloomberg.com/news/articles/2017-04-10/tesla-passes-gm-as-musk-s-carmaker-becomes-america-s-top-valued

41 Fortune 500 (2018). http://fortune.com/fortune500/tesla/

42 Muoio, D. (2017, June 26). An Ex-Tesla Exec Reveals How the Company Is Transforming Itself into a Data Powerhouse. Business Insider. Retrieved from https://www.businessinsider.sg/tesla-chris-lattner-explains-how-car-data-is-used-2017-6/

43 McKinsey (2016). Monetizing Car Data: New Service Business Opportunities to Create New Customer Benefits. Retrieved from https://www.mckinsey.com/~/media/McKinsey/Industries/Automotive%20and%20Assembly/Our%20Insights/Monetizing%20car%20data/Monetizing-car-data.ashx

44 CNN Tech (2018). Laurie Segall Interview with Tim Cook. Apple CEO: Privacy Is Fundamental Human Right. CNN Money. Retrieved from https://money.cnn.com/video/technology/2018/06/04/tim-cook-apple-privacy.cnnmoney/index.html

45 CNN Tech (2018). Laurie Segall Interview with Tim Cook. Apple CEO: Privacy Is Fundamental Human Right. CNN Money. Retrieved from https://money.cnn.com/video/technology/2018/06/04/tim-cook-apple-privacy.cnnmoney/index.html

46 Gartner (2014). Gartner Says Advanced Analytics Is a Top Business Priority. Retrieved from https://www.gartner.com/newsroom/id/2881218

47 INRIX Research (2017). Global Traffic Scorecard. Retrieved from http://inrix.com/scorecard/

48 Waze: Data, Driven Retrieved from https://www.waze.com/brands/drivers/

49 Thomas W. Malone (2018). Superminds: The Surprising Power of People and Computers Thinking Together. Little, Brown and Company, USA.

50 Abbatiello, A., Boehm, T., Schwartz, J., Chand, S. (2017). No-collar Workforce: Humans and Machines in One Loop—Collaborating in Roles and New Talent Models. Tech Trends 2018: The Symbiotic Enterprise. Deloitte University Press.

51 Guszcza, J., Lewis, H., & Evans-Greenwood, P. (2017). Cognitive collaboration: Why humans and computers think better together. Deloitte University Press.

52 World Resources Institute (2017). The Need for (Safe) Speed: 4 Surprising Ways Slower Driving Creates Better Cities. https://www.wri.org/blog/2017/05/need-safe-speed-4-surprising-ways-slower-driving-creates-better-cities

53 Gardner IT Glossary. Retrieved from https://www.gartner.com/it-glossary/descriptive-analytics/

54 Accenture (2016). What Is Descriptive Analytics? Retrieved from https://insuranceblog.accenture.com/an-introduction-to-descriptive-analytics

55 Accenture (2016). What Is Predictive Analytics? Retrieved from http://insuranceblog.accenture.com/what-is-predictive-analytics

56 McLaughlin, D. & Harris, A. M. (2017). AT&T Commits to Time Warner Deal Even as Judge Delays Deadline. Bloomberg. Retrieved from https://www.bloomberg.com/news/articles/2017-12-07/at-t-judge-says-he-will-hold-march-19-trial-on-time-warner-deal

57 Waze (2018). https://www.waze.com/

58 Hals, T., Baker, L. B. (2011). Dish Expands Its Scope with Blockbuster Win. Reuters. Retrieved from https://www.reuters.com/

article/us-blockbuster-dishnetwork/dish-expands-its-scope-with-blockbuster-win-idUSTRE7351VA20110406

59 Baker, L. B. (2013). Dish Network to Close all Blockbuster Stores, Lay off 2,800. Reuters. Retrieved from https://www.reuters.com/article/us-blockbuster-dish/dish-network-to-close-all-blockbuster-stores-lay-off-2800-idUSBRE9A511Z20131106

60 Kelleher, K. (2014). Here's Why Netflix Can Shrug Off its Stock Plunge. Time. Retrieved from http://time.com/3513855/netflix-stocks/

61 Domino's 101: Basic Facts. https://biz.dominos.com/web/public/about-dominos/fun-facts

62 Nasdaq. Historical Stock Prices. https://www.nasdaq.com/symbol/dpz/historical

63 Taylor, B. (2016). How Domino's Pizza Reinvented Itself. Harvard Business Review (HBR). https://hbr.org/2016/11/how-dominos-pizza-reinvented-itself

64 Domino's 101: Basic Facts. https://biz.dominos.com/web/public/about-dominos/fun-facts

65 Merck. Get to Know Merck. Company Fact Sheet: Employees. https://www.merck.com/about/our-history/facts/home.html

66 YCharts. Merck & Co., Inc. Historical Market Cap Data: Market Cap Range, Past 5 Years. https://ycharts.com/companies/MRK/market_cap

67 HBR IdeaCast (2018). The CEO of Merck on Race, Leadership, and High Drug Prices. Interview (Podcast) Conducted by Curt Nickisch with Ken Frazier, the CEO of Merck. Harvard Business Review (HBR). https://hbr.org/ideacast/2018/02/the-ceo-of-merck-on-race-leadership-and-high-drug-prices.html

68 Fortune 500 (2018). Merck. http://fortune.com/fortune500/merck/

69 Sonnenfeld, J. (2017). Ken Frazier: The Strongest Man in the World. Fortune. Retrieved from http://fortune.com/2017/08/15/merck-ceo-ken-frazier/

70 Fortune 500 (2018). Merck. http://fortune.com/fortune500/merck/

71 Knight, W. (2016). Microsoft Says Maverick Chatbot Tay Foreshadows the Future of Computing. MIT Technology. Retrieved

from https://www.technologyreview.com/s/601163/microsoft-says-maverick-chatbot-tay-foreshadows-the-future-of-computing/

72 Egan, M. (2017). Facebook and Amazon Hit $500 Billion Milestone. CNN Money. Retrieved from https://money.cnn.com/2017/07/27/investing/facebook-amazon-500-billion-bezos-zuckerberg/index.html

73 Berfield, S. (2014). CVS Cigarette Ban Will Drive Away $2 Billion in Sales. Blomberg. Retrieved from https://www.bloomberg.com/news/articles/2014-08-06/cvs-cigarette-ban-2-billion-in-lost-sales-and-not-just-tobbaco

74 Fortune 500 (2015). Retrieved from http://fortune.com/fortune500/2015/

75 Fortune 500 (2018). Fortune 500 Companies 2018: Who Made the List. Retrieved from http://fortune.com/fortune500/list/

76 General Data Protection Regulation (GDPR, 2016). Regulation (EU) 2016/679 of the European Parliament and of the Council. Official Journal of the European Union. Retrieved from https://eur-lex.europa.eu/legal-content/EN/TXT/PDF/?uri=CELEX:32016R0679. https://gdpr-info.eu European Commission. 2018 Reform of EU Data Protection Rules: General Data Protection Regulation (GDPR). Retrieved from https://ec.europa.eu/commission/priorities/justice-and-fundamental-rights/data-protection/2018-reform-eu-data-protection-rules_en

77 California Legislative Information. California Consumer Privacy Act: Assembly Bill (A.B.) No 375. Approved by Governor on June 28, 2018. Published on 06/29/2018. Retrieved from https://leginfo.legislature.ca.gov/faces/billTextClient.xhtml?bill_id=201720180AB375

Mason, M. (2018, June 28). Heading Off a Ballot Fight, California Lawmakers Approve Consumer Privacy Rules. Los Angeles Times. Retrieved from http://www.latimes.com/politics/essential/la-pol-ca-essential-politics-may-2018-in-effort-to-head-off-ballot-fight-1530215025-htmlstory.html

Ghosh, D. (2018). What You Need to Know About California's New Data Privacy Law. Harvard Business Review (HBR). Retrieved from https://hbr.org/2018/07/what-you-need-to-know-about-californias-new-data-privacy-law

Vartabedian, M. (2018, June 28). California Passes Sweeping Data Privacy Bill. Wall Street Journal (WSJ). Retrieved from https://www.wsj.com/articles/california-rushes-to-tighten-data-privacy-restrictions-1530190800

Adler, B. (2018, June 29). California Passes Strict Internet Privacy Law with Implications for the Country. NPR. Retrieved from https://www.npr.org/2018/06/29/624336039/california-passes-strict-internet-privacy-law-with-implications-for-the-country

78 Cavoukian Ann (2012). Privacy by Design: Origins, Meaning, and Prospects for Assuring Privacy and Trust in the Information Era.

79 Cavoukian A. (2009). Privacy by Design. Information and Privacy Commissioner of Ontario, Canada.

80 Salinas, S. & Fortt, J. (2018). Microsoft CEO Satya Nadella Says 'Trust' Will Push the Company Ahead of Amazon and Google in Cloud Computing. CNBC. Retrieved from https://www.cnbc.com/2018/05/07/microsofts-satya-nadella-trust-will-push-us-past-amazon-google.html

81 Bernard et al. (2016). Data: Bernard et al. (2016), Analyzing Qualitative Data: Systematic Approaches, 2nd Edition.

82 Bladt, J. & Filbin, B. (2013). Know the Difference Between Your Data and Your Metrics. Harvard Business Review (HBR). https://hbr.org/2013/03/know-the-difference-between-yo

83 Bladt, J. & Filbin, B. (2013). Know the Difference Between Your Data and Your Metrics. Harvard Business Review (HBR). https://hbr.org/2013/03/know-the-difference-between-yo

84 Customer Gauge (2018). 2018 NPS & CX Benchmarks Report. Conducted in Collaboration with MIT CISR, NPS Benchmarks.

85 U.S. Department of Transportation. The Bureau of Transportation Statistics: Transtats Aviation Databases. https://www.transtats.bts.gov/Databases.asp?Mode_ID=1&Mode_Desc=Aviation&Subject _ID2=0

Federation Aviation Administration (FAA): Aviation Data and Statistics. https://www.faa.gov/data_research/aviation_data_statistics/

86 Patton M.Q. (1999). Enhancing the Quality and Credibility of Qualitative Analysis. Health Service Research 34 (5) Part 2. Pp. 1189-1208.

Patton, M.Q. (2001). Qualitative Evaluation and Research Methods (2nd Edition). Thousand oaks, CA: Sage Publications.

Creswell, J.W. (1998). Qualitative Inquiry and Research Design Choosing Among Five Traditions. Thousand oaks, CA: Sage Publications. Denzin, N.K. (1978). Sociological Methods. New York: McGraw-Hill.

87 U.S. Census Bureau (1975). Historical Statistics of the United States: Colonial Times to 1970. US. Bureau of the Census. Bicentennial Edition, Part I https://www.census.gov/history/pdf/histstats-colonial-1970.pdf

88 U.S. Census Bureau. Census Day Was August 2, 1790. https://www.census.gov/history/www/through_the_decades/overview/1790.html

89 U.S. Census Bureau. Decennial Census of Population and Housing: Decennial Census Official Publications. Retrieved from https://www.census.gov/programs-surveys/decennial-census/decade/decennial-publications.1790.html

90 Sage Publications. Likert Scale. Note: "The Likert scale, named for Rensis Likert…consists of multiple items that typically are summed or averaged to produce a more reliable measure than could be obtained by use of a single item." Retrieved from http://methods.sagepub.com/reference/encyclopedia-of-survey-research-methods/n273.xml

91 Spector, P.E. (1992). Summated Rating Scale Construction: An Introduction. (Sage University Papers Series: Quantitative Applications in the Social Sciences, no. 82). Sage Publications.

92 Pew Research Center (2017). International Survey Research: International Survey Methodology. http://www.pewresearch.org/methodology/international-survey-research/international-methodology/global-attitudes-survey/mexico/2017/

93 U.S. Census Bureau. 1790 Overview: Census Day was August 2, 1790. https://www.census.gov/history/www/through_the_decades/overview/1790.html

94 Survey Monkey: Sample Size Calculator. Retrieved from https://www.surveymonkey.com/mp/sample-size-calculator/

95 Survey Monkey: Sample Size Calculator. Retrieved from https://www.surveymonkey.com/mp/sample-size-calculator/

96 Steve Jobs (2008). Apple WWDC 2008—iPhone 3G Introduction.
97 IBM. 2.5 Quintillion Bytes of Data Created Every Day. How Does CPG & Retail Manage It? Retrieved from https://www.ibm.com/blogs/insights-on-business/consumer-products/2-5-quintillion-bytes-of-data-created-every-day-how-does-cpg-retail-manage-it/
98 Christie Schneider, C. (2016). The Biggest Data Challenges That You Might Not Even Know You Have. IBM. Retrieved from https://www.ibm.com/blogs/watson/2016/05/biggest-data-challenges-might-not-even-know/
99 Henke, N., Libarikian, A., & Wiseman, B. (2016). Straight Talk About Big Data. McKinsey. Retrieved from https://www.mckinsey.com/business-functions/digital-mckinsey/our-insights/straight-talk-about-big-data
100 MIT Technology Review (2013). The Big Data Conundrum: How to Define It? Retrieved from https://www.technologyreview.com/s/519851/the-big-data-conundrum-how-to-define-it/
101 Henke, N., Libarikian, A., & Wiseman, B. (2016). Straight Talk About Big Data. McKinsey. Retrieved from https://www.mckinsey.com/business-functions/digital-mckinsey/our-insights/straight-talk-about-big-data
102 Ernst & Young (EY, 2014). Big Data: Changing the Way Businesses Compete and Operate. EY: Insights on Governance, Risk and Compliance. Retrieved from https://www.ey.com/Publication/vwLUAssets/EY_-_Big_data:_changing_the_way_businesses_operate/$FILE/EY-Insights-on-GRC-Big-data.pdf
103 NASA. Voyager 1 and 2: Mission Overview. Retrieved from https://voyager.jpl.nasa.gov/mission/
104 NASA. Your Device Has More Computing Power. Retrieved from https://www.nasa.gov/mission_pages/voyager/multimedia/vgrmemory.html#.W1eEndhKhn6
105 Salesforce IoT Cloud. The Rise of Systems of Intelligence: How the Internet of Things and Smart Systems Will Change Everything. Salesforce.
106 Stanford University. Bits and Bytes. https://web.stanford.edu/class/cs101/bits-bytes.html

107 Facebook (2018). F8 Developer Conference. https://developers.facebook.com/videos/f8-2018/f8-2018-day-1-keynote/

108 Internet Live Stats (2018): Live Reporting of Internet Statistics Per Second

109 Indiana University. Understanding Orders of Magnitude in Storage Capacity. https://kb.iu.edu/d/apeq

110 World Bank Data. Total Population. United Nations Population Division. World Population Prospects: 2017 Revision. https://data.worldbank.org/indicator/sp.pop.totl

111 Pew Research Center (2017). 10 Facts About Smartphones as the iPhone Turns 10. http://www.pewresearch.org/fact-tank/2017/06/28/10-facts-about-smartphones/

112 Statista. Exclusive Premium Statistic. Number of Smartphone Users Worldwide from 2014 to 2020. Retrieved from https://www.statista.com/statistics/330695/number-of-smartphone-users-worldwide/

113 Smith, R. (2018). IBM Created the World's First Smartphone 25 Years Ago. World Economic Forum. Retrieved from https://www.weforum.org/agenda/2018/03/remembering-first-smartphone-simon-ibm/

114 Singleton, M. (2018, June 12). The World's Fastest Supercomputer Is Back in America. The Verge. Retrieved from https://www.theverge.com/circuitbreaker/2018/6/12/17453918/ibm-summit-worlds-fastest-supercomputer-america-department-of-energy

115 Lohr, S. (2018, June 8). Move Over, China: U.S. Is Again Home to World's Speediest Supercomputer. New York Times. Retrieved from https://www.nytimes.com/2018/06/08/technology/supercomputer-china-us.html

116 The Download (2018). America's New Supercomputer Beats China's Fastest Machine to Take Title of World's Most Powerful. MIT Technology Review. Retrieved from https://www.technologyreview.com/the-download/611385/americas-new-supercomputer-beats-chinas-fastest-machine-to-take-the-worlds-most/

117 The Download (2018). America's New Supercomputer Beats China's Fastest Machine to Take Title of World's Most Powerful. MIT

Technology Review. Retrieved from https://www.technologyreview.com/the-download/611385/americas-new-supercomputer-beats-chinas-fastest-machine-to-take-the-worlds-most/

118 Henke, N., Libarikian, A., & Wiseman, B. (2016). Straight Talk About Big Data. McKinsey. Retrieved from https://www.mckinsey.com/business-functions/digital-mckinsey/our-insights/straight-talk-about-big-data

119 Calabresi, M. (2017, May). Inside Russia's Social Media War on America. Time. Retrieved from http://time.com/4783932/inside-russia-social-media-war-america/

BBC (2018). Russians Conducted 'Information Warfare' on US Election. Video of U.S. Deputy Attorney General Rosenstein. https://www.bbc.com/news/av/world-us-canada-43092569/russians-conducted-information-warfare-on-us-election

120 Branford, B. (2017, March 31). Information Warfare: Is Russia Really Interfering in European States? BBC News. Retrieved from https://www.bbc.com/news/world-europe-39401637

The Guardian (2017, April 12). Brexit: Foreign States May Have Interfered in Vote, Report Says. Retrieved from https://www.theguardian.com/politics/2017/apr/12/foreign-states-may-have-interfered-in-brexit-vote-report-says

Adam, K. & Booth, W. (2017, November 17). Rising Alarm in Britain Over Russian Meddling in Brexit Vote. Washington Post. Retrieved from https://www.washingtonpost.com/world/europe/rising-alarm-in-britain-over-russian-meddling-in-brexit-vote/2017/11/17/2e987a30-cb34-11e7-b506-8a10ed11ecf5_story.html?noredirect=on&utm_term=.3fc59ae5ca0d

121 Davenport, T. H. (2017). What's Your Data Strategy. Harvard Business Review (HBR). https://hbr.org/webinar/2017/04/whats-your-data-strategy

122 Davenport, T. H. (2017). What's Your Data Strategy. Harvard Business Review (HBR). https://hbr.org/webinar/2017/04/whats-your-data-strategy

123 NPR & Edison Research (2018). New Data: One-In-Six Americans Now Owns A Smart Speaker. National Public Media. Retrieved from

https://www.nationalpublicmedia.com/news/
smart-audio-report-winter-2017-smart-speaker-research/
NPR & Edison Research (2018). The Smart Audio Report. National Public Media. Retrieved from https://www.nationalpublicmedia.com/wp-content/uploads/2018/01/The-Smart-Audio-Report-from-NPR-and-Edison-Research-Fall-Winter-2017.pdf

124 Ericsson. The Connected Future. Internet of Things Forecast. Retrieved from https://www.ericsson.com/en/mobility-report/internet-of-things-forecast

125 Satya Nadella (2018). Opportunity and Responsibility in the Era of the Intelligent Cloud and Intelligent Edge. LinkedIn. Retrieved from https://www.linkedin.com/pulse/opportunity-responsibility-era-intelligent-cloud-edge-satya-nadella/

126 GPMG (2017). Governing the Bot Revolution: How Centralized Control Stops Ad Hoc RPA Deployment and Drives True Transformation. Racing Ahead with RPA. Retrieved from https://advisory.kpmg.us/articles/2017/governing-bot-revolution.html

127 GPMG (2017). Governing the Bot Revolution: How Centralized Control Stops Ad Hoc RPA Deployment and Drives True Transformation. Racing Ahead with RPA. Retrieved from https://advisory.kpmg.us/articles/2017/governing-bot-revolution.html

128 McKinsey (2016). Digital McKinsey. The Next Acronym You Need to Know About: (RPA (Robotic Process Automation). Interview Conducted by Xavier Lhuer, Associate Principal at McKinsey, with Leslie Willcocks, Professor of Technology, Work, and Globalization at the London School of Economics' Department of Management. Retrieved from https://www.mckinsey.com/business-functions/digital-mckinsey/our-insights/the-next-acronym-you-need-to-know-about-rpa

129 Salem H., Roth E., & Fornango J. (1983). A Comparison of Automated Data Collection and Manual Data Collection for Toxicology Studies. Archives of Toxicology, volume 6. https://www.ncbi.nlm.nih.gov/m/pubmed/6578744/

130 Lucker, J., Hogan, S. K., & Bischoff, T. (2017). Predictably Inaccurate: The Prevalence and Perils of Bad Big Data. Deloitte Review, issue 21.

https://www2.deloitte.com/insights/us/en/deloitte-review/issue-21/analytics-bad-data-quality.html
131 IBM Big Data Analytics Hub. Infographics Animations: The Four V's of Big Data. IBM. Retrieved from https://www.ibmbigdatahub.com/infographic/four-vs-big-data
132 Chakravorti, B. & Chaturvedi, R. S. (2017). Digital Planet 2017: How Competitiveness and Trust in Digital Economies Vary Across the World. The Fletcher School, Tufts University.
https://sites.tufts.edu/digitalplanet/executive-summary/
https://sites.tufts.edu/digitalplanet/files/2017/05/Digital_Planet_2017_FINAL.pdf
133 KPMG (2017). Ten Key Regulatory Challenges for 2018: Actions to Drive Effective Change in Financial Services. KPMG. https://assets.kpmg.com/content/dam/kpmg/us/pdf/2018/02/728013-nss-fs-top-10v5-web.pdf
134 CNN Tech (2018). Steve Jobs Warned About Privacy Issues in 2010. Mark Zuckerberg Was in the Audience. CNN Money. Retrieved from https://money.cnn.com/2018/03/27/technology/steve-jobs-mark-zuckerberg-privacy-2010/index.html
135 Netflix. Black Mirror S4:E1 "USS Callister"
136 Fortune 500. Note: In 2017, "*Fortune* 500 companies represent two-thirds of the U.S. GDP with $12.8 trillion in revenues, $1.0 trillion in profits, $21.6 trillion in market value, and employ 28.2 million people worldwide." Retrieved from http://fortune.com/fortune500/

Fortune Global 500. Note: "The world's 500 largest companies generated $30 trillion in revenues and $1.9 trillion in profits in 2017. Together, this year's Fortune Global 500 companies employ 67.7 million people worldwide and are represented by 33 countries." Retrieved from http://fortune.com/global500/
137 Vartabedian, M. (2018, June 28). California Passes Sweeping Data Privacy Bill. Wall Street Journal (WSJ). Retrieved from https://www.wsj.com/articles/
california-rushes-to-tighten-data-privacy-restrictions-1530190800
138 Bell, K. (2018, May 13). Tim Cook: 2018 Duke University Commencement Speech. Mashable. https://mashable.

com/2018/05/14/tim-cook-duke-commencement-speech-2018/#Qu_pnQRFQmqu

139 Tufts University. Office of the Vice Provost for Research: Social, Behavioral & Educational Research. Institutional Review Board (IRB). Protocol Application Process. https://viceprovost.tufts.edu/sberirb/researcher-responsibilities/ http://web.tufts.edu/central/research/msword/Medford/SBER_IRB_Brochure_2007-2008.pdf

U.S. Department of Health & Human Services. Office of Human Research Protection. Regulations, Policy, & Posting. Human Subject Regulations Decision Charts. https://www.hhs.gov/ohrp/regulations-and-policy/decision-charts/index.html

140 Apple. 5.1 Privacy. https://developer.apple.com/app-store/review/guidelines/#privacy

141 European Union (EU). General Data Protection Regulation (GDPR). https://europa.eu/youreurope/business/sell-abroad/data-protection/index_en.htm

142 European Commission (2017, April 4): When Is a Data Protection Impact Assessment (DPIA) Required? European Commission. Regulation (EU) 2016/679 https://ec.europa.eu/info/law/law-topic/data-protection/reform/rules-business-and-organisations/obligations/when-data-protection-impact-assessment-dpia-required_en

143 European Union (EU). General Data Protection Regulation (GDPR). https://europa.eu/youreurope/business/sell-abroad/data-protection/index_en.htm

144 UNCTAD (2016). Data Protection Regulations and International Data Flows: Implications for Trade and Development. UN Publications: UNCTAD/DTL/STICT/2016/1. http://unctad.org/en/PublicationsLibrary/dtlstict2016d1_en.pdf

145 Shearer, E. & Gottfried, J. (2017). News Use Across Social Media Platforms 2017. Pew Research Center. Retrieved from http://www.journalism.org/2017/09/07/news-use-across-social-media-platforms-2017/

146 Grieco, E. (2017). More Americans Are Turning to Multiple Social Media Sites For News. Pew Research Center. Retrieved from http://www.pewresearch.org/fact-tank/2017/11/02/more-americans-are-turning-to-multiple-social-media-sites-for-news/

Shearer, E. & Gottfried, J. (2017). News Use Across Social Media Platforms 2017. Pew Research Center. Retrieved from http://www.journalism.org/2017/09/07/news-use-across-social-media-platforms-2017/

147 U.S. Congress (2018). Testimony of Mr. Greg Brockman, co-founder of Open AI, a Non-profit Artificial Intelligence Development Organization. https://docs.house.gov/meetings/SY/SY15/20180626/108474/HHRG-115-SY15-Wstate-BrockmanG-20180626.pdf

148 United Nations Development Group (UNDP, 2017). Data Privacy, Ethics and Protection: Guidance Note on Big Data for Achievement of the 2030 Agenda.

149 McKinsey (2016). Digital Globalization: The New Era of Global Flows. https://www.mckinsey.com/~/media/McKinsey/Business%20Functions/McKinsey%20Digital/Our%20Insights/Digital%20globalization%20The%20new%20era%20of%20global%20flows/MGI-Digital-globalization-Full-report.ashx

150 United Nations Conference on Trade and Development (UNCTAD, 2018). Data Protection and Privacy Legislation Worldwide: http://unctad.org/en/Pages/DTL/STI_and_ICTs/ICT4D-Legislation/eCom-Data-Protection-Laws.aspx

151 United Nations Conference on Trade and Development (UNCTAD, 2018). Cybercrime Legislation Worldwide: http://unctad.org/en/Pages/DTL/STI_and_ICTs/ICT4D-Legislation/eCom-Cybercrime-Laws.aspx

152 United Nations Conference on Trade and Development (UNCTAD, 2018). Data Protection and Privacy Legislation Worldwide: http://unctad.org/en/Pages/DTL/STI_and_ICTs/ICT4D-Legislation/eCom-Data-Protection-Laws.aspx

153 United Nations (UN). Universal Declaration of Human Rights, article 12.

154 United Nations Department of Economic and Social Affairs (UN DESA).
https://www.un.org/development/desa/en/about/organigramme.html

155 Facebook (2018). Newsroom Statistics. https://newsroom.fb.com/company-info/

156 Facebook (2018). F8 Developers Conference. https://developers.facebook.com/videos/f8-2018/f8-2018-day-1-keynote/

157 U.S. Census Bureau (2015). Census Bureau Reports at Least 350 Languages Spoken in U.S. Homes. https://www.census.gov/newsroom/press-releases/2015/cb15-185.html

158 Ethnologue. Explore the World's Languages. Retrieved from https://www.ethnologue.com. https://www.ethnologue.com/browse/names

159 Boudette, N. E. (2018, June 30). Inside Tesla's Audacious Push to Reinvent the Way Cars Are Made. New York Times. Retrieved from https://www.nytimes.com/2018/06/30/business/tesla-factory-musk.html

160 CBS This Morning (2018). Rare Look Inside Tesla's Model 3 Factory. Interview with Gayle King during a tour of Tesla's Factory. CBS News. Retrieved from https://www.cbs.com/shows/cbs_this_morning/video/FMN4XL5kYziyfOOgz_QcKARo7NWm0Gsf/tesla-ceo-elon-musk-offers-rare-look-inside-model-3-factory/

161 Twitter (2018, April 13). Elon Musk: Tweet in Response to Tim Higgins, a *Wall Street Journal* (WSJ) Technology and Auto Reporter.

162 Abbatiello, A., Boehm, T., Schwartz, J., Chand, S. (2017). No-collar Workforce: Humans and Machines in One Loop—Collaborating in Roles and New Talent Models. Tech Trends 2018: The Symbiotic Enterprise. Deloitte University Press.

About the Author

Journel Joseph is a multi-disciplinary, multilingual, data and analytics professional, with over a decade of industry and consulting experience. His expertise is focused on data visualization, structured and unstructured data, predictive analytics, observational studies, quantitative and qualitative research methods, digital strategy, quality control, data privacy and policy. He also has a keen interest in artificial intelligence, machine learning, blockchain, virtual and augmented reality technologies.

Journel currently functions as a data scientist based in Washington, D.C., providing data integration, preparation, visualization, and building predictive models, in addition to analytics solutions on government contracting and corporate research projects. He is the founder of Insert Analytics; a startup data and analytics advisory firm specializing in the design and implementation of customized solutions in advanced analytics, visualization, digital strategy, machine intelligence and data privacy.

Journel is a graduate of the Fletcher School of Law and Diplomacy at Tufts University with a Master of International Affairs degree where he specialized in Economics, and International Trade. In addition, he has a Master of Public Policy degree from the Department of Urban and Environmental Policy and Planning (UEP), Graduate School of Arts and Sciences at Tufts University. He holds a bachelor's degree in Technology and Community Media from the University of Massachusetts and he has completed a 2-year NSF-funded training in Program Evaluation and Applied Research. He holds an Advanced Graduate Certificate in Program Evaluation from Tufts University.

Made in the USA
Monee, IL
04 November 2026

67387165R00154